The Complete Book of

SILK SCREEN PRINTING PRODUCTION

by

J. I. BIEGELEISEN

Production Manager, Paint Print Process Company
Chairman, Art Department, High School of Art and Design
New York

With an Introduction by

CARL S. AUERBACH

SCI Division of Communications Affiliates, Inc.

Dover Publications, Inc.

New York

Published in Canada by General Publishing Com-
pany, Ltd., 30 Lesmill Road, Don Mills, Toronto,
Ontario.
Published in the United Kingdom by Constable
and Company, Ltd., 10 Orange Street, London
WC 2.

*The Complete Book of Silk Screen Printing Pro-
duction* is a new work, first published by Dover
Publications, Inc. in 1963.

Standard Book Number: 486-21100-2
Library of Congress Catalog Card Number: 63-17898

Manufactured in the United States of America
Dover Publications, Inc.
180 Varick Street
New York, N.Y. 10014

INTRODUCTION

I like silk screen printing.

I like it because, in thirty years of graphic arts activity, I have never seen any other process which can offer the depth and richness of color that can be achieved by silk screen.

I suppose this is something like saying that I like clear skies, Brigitte Bardot, Babe Ruth, and $10,000 convertibles. It is nonetheless sincere and honest.

We live today in a world of color. Our clothing, cars, and homes all reflect the color consciousness which has become a hallmark of the twentieth century. In supermarkets and department stores, on TV and on billboards, in magazines and in newspapers there is one dominant common denominator—color.

In past years color was used to come as close as possible to nature's own creations. Today our ladies tint their hair, their eyes and their lips and their fingertips in colors that swing far away from the natural colors, and we love it.

We use color for beauty, as above; for sales appeal in our packaging; for attention arresting as in our traffic signs; for mood induction in our draperies and furniture. And when the time comes that we must reproduce these extravagant colors in the graphic arts, we turn with most certainty to silk screen process.

In theory, application, and practice there is no reason why silk screen should not be the best method of laying color on a carrier. Whether that carrier be paper, glass, metal, or plastic, the basic concept of silk screen which involves the simple physical application of ink directly onto the surface to be printed is a method which brooks no failure.

Such being the case, we are pleased to be associated with any-thing concerning the art of silk screen process, and feel that every-one connected with the graphic arts should know the range of its application and the extent of its capabilities. This book does that job quite completely.

To those of us who have an acquaintance with the silk screen field, there is no better source of this know-how than Jack Biegeleisen, whose years in this field have brought him up against every problem and almost every solution that can arise. The hours, days, and, months that he has spent assembling this handbook are limitless. His reward will come from your close attention to his wonderfully coherent explanation of silk screen work.

In a world of color consciousness silk screen plays a vital role. We would all do well to know as much about it as possible. Those who read this book will be among the well-informed.

CARL S. AUERBACH

SCI Division of

Communications Affiliates, Inc.

New York, 1963

PREFACE

AN INDUSTRY as rapidly growing as screen process ofttimes makes present techniques and equipment obsolete within a short time. I must confess that when I began writing this book I did so not without a wavering reluctance in mentioning specific products by their commercial trade names. I could not help but be sensitive to a lingering doubt or fear that the material in the book might go into obsolescence along with the techniques and products mentioned. I felt, too, that some doubt might also arise in the reader's mind concerning my personal partiality in mentioning some trade names in preference to others. It would have been easy to resolve all these mental conflicts by mentioning no brand names at all since I could not possibly mention them all. Such an apparently scholarly position, however, would not prove to be of service to the reader, since a good many of these trade names have promise of durability and have in fact become, at least for the time being, synonymous with the products which they represent. Some may not fulfill that promise and may be eventually replaced by new favorites.

I hope in future revisions of this book to review the scene as it will appear at that time and bring the information up to date to reflect conditions as they will be then.

And now about how this book originated.

What started out as a revision of one of my books published in 1941 has ended as a new book. I have made no more use of my own book as reference material than I have of other literature in the field. This included the excellent books written by my professional colleagues Bert Zahn, Albert Kosloff, Bob Fossett, and others, as well as the authoritative manuals compiled by the Screen Process Printing Association, International. In addition, I have consulted with and received the whole-hearted cooperation of the prominent suppliers in the field who are listed elsewhere in the book under the heading of "Sources of Supply." To all those, I owe my gratitude.

My knowledge of the subject is, however, not limited to reading about it in books or consulting with others. My own personal experience as a daily practitioner in the field goes back more than twenty-five years, and extends to the present day. During my long internship I have had occasion to work in every department of the screen shop: as printer, paint mixer, layout and lettering artist, stencil man, manager, estimator and consultant. Concurrently with these practical experiences, I have managed to publish three previous books on the process; I have organized classes in silk screen in the New York City high schools; and I now supervise the screen department of the High School of Art and Design where I serve as Chairman of the Art Department.

I sincerely hope that the rather broad knowledge that I have acquired during this long period may be reflected in the manner in which the factual material has been presented in this book.

J. I. BIEGELEISEN

New York, 1963

CONTENTS

1. BRIEF HISTORY OF THE PROCESS

IT IS too bad that the discovery of the silk screen process cannot be associated with some heroic figure of the legendary stature of a Gutenberg or a Senefelder. There is a definite date marking Gutenberg's historic discovery of movable type. The year was 1450. Senefelder is said to have stumbled on the accidental discovery of lithography by writing a laundry ticket on a grease-coated stone, back in 1796. As for silk screen, it has no classic and definite heritage. No godfather attended its christening. No indisputable record has been traced to mark its date or place of origin. Perhaps it may be best to console oneself by saying that though the process may have had a vague past, it has a brilliant future. It is now generally recognized as one of the major graphic arts along with letterpress, lithography and gravure. And the commercial process as we know it today actually started only sixty years ago.

Though no one man's name or no one place of origin is credited with the discovery of silk screen, there are writers in the field who attribute the process (in its earliest form) to the ancient Chinese and Egyptians, who employed open stencils for applying ornamental decorations to fabrics, wallpaper and walls. Their stencils were not really silk stencils; rather they were sheets of impervious materials cut to form an open design. Dyes and other media were brushed over the openings of the stencil, resulting in a facsimile "print." The nearest early prototype of the method employed today of which we have positive evidence were the stencils made by the early Japanese—a method which has continued until the advent

1

of the stencil mounted on silk (the beginning of the screen process as we know it today). The Japanese stencils consisted of oil-treated heavy paper sheets through which openings were cut in rather intricate detail. To keep the isolated parts of the cut paper from dropping out, the Japanese printmaker painstakingly glued a spider-like network of human hair across the openings, thus keeping all of the integral parts of the stencil intact.

The method of cutting stencil openings on impervious sheets, such as oiled paper, metal, etc., has been known and used by many peoples throughout the centuries. Up to this very day, decorations and lettering are still applied to walls, simple sign boards and packing crates in that way. This type of stencil is characterized by little ties or bridges of the stencil tissue which keep the island parts of the design suspended. A print made with such a stencil shows gaps or breaks which interrupt the continuity of the design.

In a way, the early Japanese hair-crossed stencil may be considered the antecedent of modern silk screen. The Japanese stencil maker did not use conspicuous ties in his design structure. The strands of human hair which held the isolated parts in suspension were so fine that their presence was hardly discernible in the finished print. The loose paint brushed over the stencil flooded the openings sufficiently to result in a continuous unbroken design.

The principle of using an invisible web of strands of hair as a carrier or screen for the stencil image (in order to eliminate conspicuous ties) was the forerunner of the modern screen stencil. The silk screen today is, after all, nothing more than a ready-made web or meshwork of strands, not of human hair, but of finely woven silk threads. Experimental work using woven silk as a screen was done in Germany and France as far back as 1870 and was then carried on in England. It is a matter of record that a patent related to silk screen was granted in 1907 to a Samuel Simon of Manchester, England. The Simon patent covered the use of the screen as a carrier for the stencil but it did not include a squeegee. Simon used a bristle brush instead of a squeegee to force the paint through the silk.

Although the process had its uncertain beginnings in China, Japan, Germany, France and England, it is in America that it was first developed and exploited as a commercial craft.

In America, though no one man was granted any controlling patent on the basic principle, much activity in the development of the process took place on the West Coast. In 1914, a multicolor screen process was perfected by a commercial artist named John Pilsworth of San Francisco, who later, in collaboration with a Mr. Owens, was granted a patent for screening several colors from a single screen. This was known and commercialized as the Selectasine method and was developed into a thriving business.

From California, the use of the process spread eastward. At first, it was looked upon as a tedious process requiring too much painstaking effort for practical commercial work. During the teeming activity of World War I, the process was taken up by sign painters and decorators of flags, pennants and banners. At first, the intricacies of the process were kept under cover, shared only by a select few. Any new developments, such as the photographic and tusche methods, were jealously guarded as "house secrets." These "secrets" in time became public property emerging into a fledgling industry, which was soon competing with the craft of sign painting and showcard writing. With the growth of chain stores from mere groups of four or five to twenty or thirty or more stores, the individually hand-lettered signs soon gave way to the process whereby identical signs could be mechanically duplicated in any desired quantity. As a consequence, the very sign writers who at first looked upon the process as a competitive craft began to adopt and experiment with it themselves. Many of them abandoned hand lettering altogether in favor of silk screen printing as a new and profitable specialty.

Thus the method became popularized, but unfortunately not popular with national advertisers of high-level merchandising. Compared to lithography and letterpress, the results obtained by silk screen were crude. The prints lacked quality as well as uniformity. They were identified by blurry, ragged edges. The paints used were home-made and often failed to dry. Production was at a snail's pace. An automatic screen printing press was patented in 1925 but was not adopted by the processors. The trouble was that the screen paints used in those days dried too slowly to keep up with the output of the machine. The machine produced faster work, but the quality of the prints was no better than that achieved with the manual printing units. Advertising agencies for the most part wanted no part of the process since the results did not measure up to the standards of highly developed lithographic or letterpress methods.

A milestone in the process was reached in 1929. In that year, in Dayton, Ohio, a screen printer named Louis F. D'Autremont developed a knife-cut stencil film tissue which was patented by an associate, A. S. Danemon. They called this film tissue Profilm. At first they used it in their own print shop, and later marketed it for national distribution. With the use of this knife-cut film tissue, it was possible to overcome one of the important drawbacks to the process; namely, the ragged unsharp print quality which had heretofore been associated with silk screen. It is true that even at that time and before, screens could be made photographically with acceptable sharpness and fidelity of line, but the photographic method was cumbersome and as yet undeveloped. It was the introduction of Profilm, therefore, which made the process take a new turn.

Several years later, Joe Ulano, a young man who was at that time a foreman in a New York screen shop developed a film which he patented as Nufilm. This patent was contested in the courts by the manufacturers of Profilm. Ulano lost the verdict, but won the prize. He was to become a licensee of the Profilm Company, but in a short time so perfected his own film that it was widely accepted as the standard here and abroad. The Ulano Nufilm was easier to cut, adhered more easily to the silk, and was more efficient time-wise, than the original Profilm.

This favorable turn in the development of the industry has served as an inducement for important paint manufacturers to look upon the process as a good potential market for specially formulated paints. Heretofore, the total dollar value of business for paint manufacturers was not attractive enough to be taken seriously. Now, efforts are made to formulate complete lines of paints for screening on paper, board, glass, textiles, and every other one of the growing number of printing surfaces to which the process could be applied. Heretofore, the paints used in silk screen were for the most part self-formulated mixtures of coach or japan colors, crudely ground pigments, lithographic oils and other compounds not refined for the process. These colors required hours of drying in racks. Indeed, some obstinately refused to dry at all—and production of printing was geared to the drying time! Today, paints and other compounds are formulated to air dry within ten minutes or force dry within seconds.

As a consequence, or perhaps concomitantly, there has for the last fifteen years been an awakened interest in fast automatic screen presses capable of production speeds of 2000 to 3000 impressions an hour. These presses work in tandem with conveyers and drying ovens where the prints are ejected and stacked—all without human effort or physical exertion. Although the trend towards automation is presently going on at a rapid rate, it is safe to predict that standardized automatic screen presses will never completely replace the manually operated printing units. It is interesting to note that many screen printing establishments which have automatic equipment on the floor very often still resort to hand-operated equipment. Why? The answer will be evident in the following statement of facts.

One of the selling features of screen process is that it can print on *any* material, *any* size, *any* thickness of stock, *any* color compound, *any* quantity. Five "any's." One need not be an M.I.T. graduate to figure out that one type of machine could not possibly do all that. While it is true that there are special machines to do each type of work, one machine cannot be that flexible. Take the matter of size. With screen process, it is possible to print a short run of five hundred cloth banners, each twenty feet long. The wooden screen frame, which is comparatively easy and inexpensive to construct, is built to accommodate the corresponding dimensions of the job. It may prove practical to construct this special printing frame even if the equipment is not intended to be used again for a long time—or ever. It would take a colossal mechanical leviathan to produce this jumbo-sized job by machine. The quickness by which a screen frame is constructed makes it possible for the processor to accept a versatile type of work, size-wise.

There are special automatic machines for printing on cylindrical objects. There are some excellent machines for screening decalcomanias which may also be used for printing on other thin stocks. That is, again, fine for the specialist. However, the average processor is no specialist. His facilities must be easily adaptable to any type of work which comes his way. Therefore, he cannot eliminate hand-printing units because in so doing he diminishes his versatility. The average processor will gradually introduce some mechanical automatic equipment but at the same time hold on to the flexible manual equipment whereby he can render a broad service to his customers. However, it is none the less true that with the continued development of better and faster automatic screening and drying equipment, the industry will branch off into specialties. That is happening already. There are organizations blueprinted and set up solely for screening 24-sheet posters, others which do nothing but ceramic ware, or wallpaper, or container printing, or metal signs or one of a multitude of other fabricating specialties.

It is a credit to American ingenuity that the United States, which was historically late in entering the field of screen printing, has taken the lead in converting a crude hand craft into a major industry with an output of over three hundred million dollars per year.

This lead is not only in terms of annual output or number of people employed. It applies equally well to organizational ability in education and industrial cohesiveness. The Screen Process Printing Association, International (S.P.P.A.), organized in the United States in 1948, represents the keystone of the industry the world over. The annual conventions are attended by processors from every land where the process is employed. This world-wide trade organization has brought together "competitors" and caused them to work together on an amicable basis, to raise the prestige of the industry through technical research and good public relations with the advertising industry. The S.P.P.A. International's periodical literature and published manuals, widely distributed to members and schools, represent the best in collective thinking and recorded data on the technical developments in the field. Textbooks on the subject by such outstanding practitioners as Bert Zahn, Harry Hiett and Albert Kosloff have helped immeasurably to popularize the process among those whose curiosity in the subject was a natural prerequisite for instructional help. I should like to feel that I, too, have helped in this respect through the authorship of several textbooks in the field. *Screen Process Magazine*, the official trade magazine, is distributed the world over and has helped to acquaint the public with new developments in techniques and materials. Courses in screen process are now offered in many high schools and colleges.

Bouquets should also be extended to the many suppliers in the field—ink makers, machine builders and photo technicians, for their part in helping to nurse this infant industry through its swaddling days and fostering its growth to the status of a respected adult member in the family of graphic arts.

2. BASIC EQUIPMENT AND TOOLS

IT HAS been said that you can start in the screen process business on a "shoe string." Perhaps there are "strings" attached to that assertion since, as we shall see in a later chapter, automation is slowly changing the complexion of this business from a simple manual craft to a big industrial enterprise. It is true, however, that the basic printing equipment necessary to get started is simple and far less costly than for any other comparative commercial printing process you can name. The basic working screen printing unit consists of a silk-stretched frame, hinged to a flat board which is its printing base. That, and a rubber squeegee, comprise the "press." While this is theoretically true, however, the average screen processor doing commercial work expands his inventory of equipment and enlarges his production facilities to include most of the items mentioned in this chapter. Let us review the major areas of equipment by categories, such as screen frames, printing bases, squeegees, hand tools and accessories, etc.

SCREEN FRAMES

The screen frame may be made of wood or metal. By far the greater number of frames used in manual printing are made of wood.

Wood Frames

The wood frame consists of four pieces of 1″ x 2″ strong, knot-free wood, rigidly constructed so as to be free from corner twists.

Wood strips selected may be spruce, cypress or white pine. The wood must be free from warpage; it must be well-sanded and preferably of kiln-dried stock. The thickness of the frame strips is not fixed. A larger frame will require heavier wood to withstand

FIG. 1. Half lap joint corner con-struction of screen frame.

FIG. 2. Tongue and groove joint cor-ner construction of screen frame.

the proportionately greater pull of the silk. Figures 1 and 2 show several interlocking corner joints recommended for rigidity in

FIG. 3. Grooved frame used with wedge cord for holding silk to wood frame without the use of tacks or staples.

professional screen frame construction. Figure 3 shows a special type of grooved frame. This type of screen frame requires no tacks or staples; instead, it is designed to be used with a special cord which is wedged into the groove, thus holding the silk in a hoop-like manner. This frame is mentioned further in Chapter 8.

Metal Frames

Various types of machine-tooled metal frames are available.

These are more widely used in standard sizes to fit frame carriages on automatic screen presses. Metal frames are considerably heavier than wood and much more costly, but they have the advantage of rigidity, an important factor in close tolerance register. They are also used frequently with special stretching devices for stainless steel screens employed for screening cylindrical ware, circuitry and other industrial printing jobs.

Floating-bar Frames

The single "floating bar" (Figure 4) consists of an additional strip of wood or metal of the same thickness as the frame, placed inside the frame crosswise, about 2″ from the end. One edge of the stencil fabric is attached to the floating bar instead of to the outer side of the frame. Long screw bolts extend from the ends of the floating bar through holes in the frame and project about one inch beyond the end of the frame. Wing nuts are screwed on the ends of the bolts. To stretch the fabric, the wing nuts are tightened.

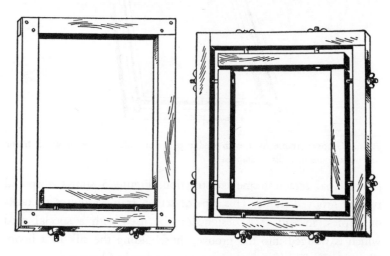

FIG. 4. Single floating bar frame.   FIG. 5. Full floating bar frame.

Figure 5 shows a full floating bar, using the same principle on all four sides of the screen.

Figure 6 shows a special frame which is widely used in automatic screen presses. This one, called the General "Seri-Chase," is a frame made of hardwood with metal holding devices on all four sides. Metal rods are passed through hems on each side of the fabric and inserted in the holding devices. The fabric then can be tightened by the turn of thumb screws on each side of the chase. These thumb

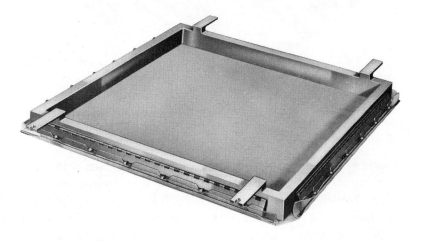

FIG. 6. Special metal frame used on some automatic presses. (*Courtesy General Research, Inc.*)

screws make it possible to adjust the fabric to drum tightness and keep it taut.

Pneumatic Screen Frames

Figure 7 shows a novel type of frame which works on the principle of an expanding tire. After the fabric is loosely attached to special gripping strips, the frame is inflated, and in expanding draws the fabric taut. Pneumatic frames are reserved mostly for stainless steel and other difficult-to-stretch metal screen fabrics.

PRINTING BASE

The simplest type of printing base is a thick, smooth, flat board, free from warpage and larger all around than the screen frame

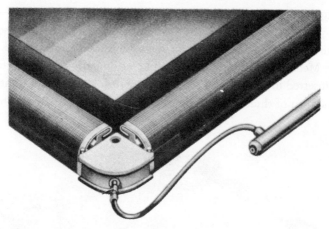

FIG. 7. Corner view of expanding frame which works on the pneumatic principle. The tube around the aluminum frame is encased in mesh in this model. (*Courtesy American Screen Process Equipment Co.*)

which will be hinged to it. It has been found, however, that better printing results are achievable when using a perforated base with a motor-driven vacuum suction action. This is especially desirable for printing on paper and other thin stock. The action of the vacuum holds the printing stock down on the base, keeping the stock from sticking to the underside of the screen. All modern automatic presses use vacuum printing base-table units.

Hinges

The frame is attached to the base by means of a set of male and female hinges. Figure 8 shows a simple type of hinge commonly known as a push-pin hinge. The pin is removed to disengage the screen frame from the base.

Figure 9 shows another type known as a hinge clamp.

Figure 10 shows a hinge device, trade-mark identified as "Magic Hand." This is a hinge-base setup which not only hinge-clamps the screen to the base, but may adjust it to various angles when desired. The rods on either end are to prevent side-to-side sway.

Counterbalances

The screen must be kept at an elevated position for the feeding

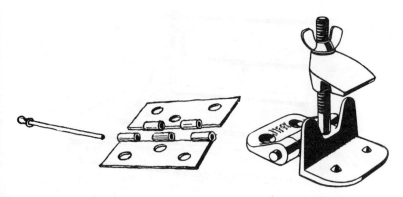

FIG. 8. Push-pin hinges, male and female, and interlocking pins.

FIG. 9. Hinge clamp.

FIG. 10. "Magic Hand" hinge base set. (*Courtesy Kenn Equipment Co.*)

and removing of the stock. Figures 11 to 15 show several systems which fulfill the purpose intended. These systems are generally

FIG. 11. Back pulley counterbalance.

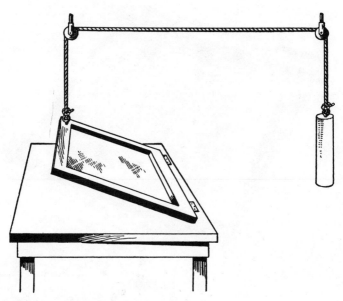

FIG. 12. Overhead pulley counterbalance.

used for manually operated printing units. Automatic presses have built-in devices for raising and lowering the screen intermittently.

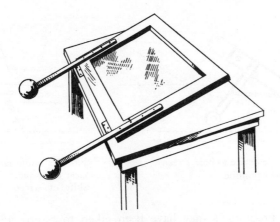

FIG. 13. Lever weight counterbalance.

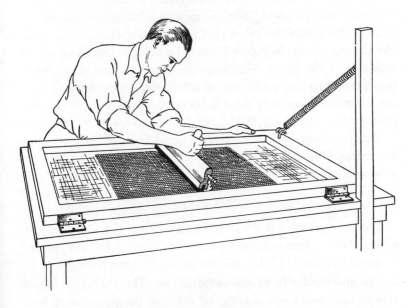

FIG. 14. Position for squeegeeing.

Locking Screen Cleats

It is imperative that there be no side-to-side twist to the hinged screen. If there were, accurate registration would not be possible.

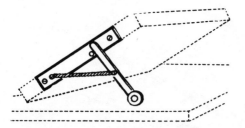

FIG. 15. Simple device to hold screen frame in raised position.

FIG. 16. Adjustable screen cleat to prevent side-to-side shift of screen frame.

Although precautions may have been taken to assure rigidity of frame construction and tightness of clamp or hinge attachments, there still may be some "give" or imperceptible side-to-side movement of the screen. To offset that possibility, a cleat arrangement like the one shown in Figure 16 may be helpful. One is affixed to each side of the frame. The frame fits snugly within these cleats, thus preventing any possibility of side-to-side sway. Another way, not illustrated here, is to drive a heavy nail or dowel through the front side of the screen frame, right down to $\frac{1}{8}''$ into the base. The nail or dowel will always interlock, thus assuring a sway-free movement. Objections to this are that both the frame and base are somewhat mutilated in the process.

SQUEEGEES

The squeegee used in screen printing consists of a heavy strip of rubber bolted between two pieces of wood with the rubber projecting about $1\frac{1}{4}''$ beyond the wood. Rubber belting can be bought independently of the wood holder. The rubber comes in various thicknesses in a number of different compositions of both natural and synthetic rubber. A new kind of plastic "rubber" composition is available which is said to have these advantages among others: it retains its resiliency indefinitely, hardly ever wears out its edge and can be used with almost any type of printing compound without any detrimental chemical effect.

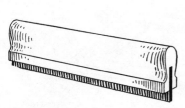

FIG. 17. Two-hand squeegee.   FIG. 18. One-hand squeegee.

The flexibility of rubber is measured in terms of durometers. Sixty-durometer rubber is used for general work. Softer rubber (forty or fifty durometers) is used to get a heavier deposit, for textile printing and uneven surfaces. Hard rubber (seventy or eighty durometers) will print sharper, produce a thinner ink film and retain its edge longer. The latter is used extensively for machine operation.

There are several kinds of squeegees. Figure 17 shows the two-hand type. Here, pressure is applied in printing by grasping the squeegee firmly with both hands for equalized distribution of pressure. Figure 18 shows the one-hand squeegee with a center handle or grip. Here the squeegee is manipulated by applying pressure with one hand. The handle is detachable, and so are the wood side pieces which hold the rubber. When the squeegee rubber has worn down on one side, it may be taken out of the wood casing, reversed, and thus made ready for another long period of service.

Figure 19 shows a typical manually operated unit, screen hinged to the base, guides set in position, cleats attached and squeegee set in position for printing. Pins set on the sides of the squeegee prevent the squeegee from falling over into the screen.

Figure 20 shows the "One-man squeegee" unit with counterweight. More will be said on this type of squeegee in the chapter on automation (Chapter 16).

Squeegee Sharpener

The squeegee rubber is extremely durable and will hold its edge

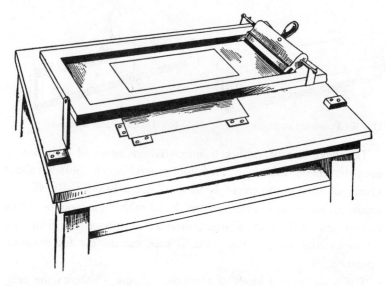

FIG. 19. Simple stencil printing unit showing squeegee in position, registry guides, frame cleats, and drop leg for frame support.

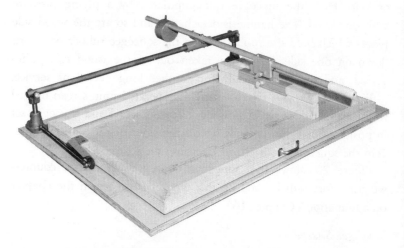

FIG. 20. "One-man squeegee," the simplest of the semi-automatic printing units. (*Courtesy M & M Research Engineering Co.*)

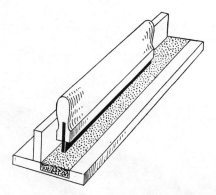

FIG. 21. Simple sandpaper block jig for sharpening squeegees.

for thousands of sharp impressions. When the edge wears down finally, it may be revived by sanding it down.

Figure 21 shows a sandpaper block jig set up as a "planer" for sharpening. The squeegee is moved evenly across the abrasive surface until the edge is renewed. Figure 22 shows an electrical sanding unit which will accomplish the same purpose faster and more uniformly.

RACKS

With the constant improvement in paint formulation to accelerate the drying of paints and other printing compounds, and with oven-drying systems, print drying is no longer the problem it used to be. However, not all shops are as yet equipped with drying ovens, nor do all paints dry quite fast enough to do away with the need for individual racking. It is still necessary to rack slow-drying prints by placing them in drying racks. There are a number of such racking systems in use which we will discuss.

Festoon Racking

Figure 23 shows a system for racking long banners or other flexible sheeted material. This device consists merely of two wooden

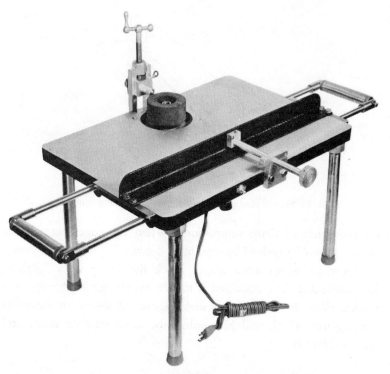

FIG. 22. Electrical sanding unit for sharpening squeegees. (*Courtesy Naz-Dar Co.*)

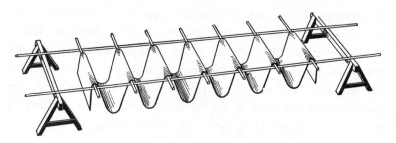

FIG. 23. Festoon arrangement for drying long lengths of flexible material.

horses on which are placed two long strips of wood acting as supporting rails for cross-ties. Being movable, these ties may be spread out or condensed as the occasion requires. This is often referred to as "festoon" racking and is used in cloth and wallpaper work. A system of festoon racking may be rigged up so that the entire unit can be elevated off the floor.

Rolling-rack Unit

This type of rack used to be standard equipment in all screen shops. It is still to be found in most shops, even those that are equipped with automatic drying ovens. Enamels and other slow-drying paints which do not oven-dry fast enough are placed in these racks. They are also useful for drying glass, masonite, and various other materials. These racks are generally custom made to the required specifications. A practical size is one that measures 72″ high, 65″ wide, and 40″ deep. Wooden strips 1″ wide and ½″ thick are used for cross-pieces. The rack should be equipped with casters so that the unit, empty or loaded, can be wheeled freely (Figure 24).

Speed Rack

This is similar to the rolling rack but it has one important special feature. The rack shelves are not fixed. Each shelf can be lifted to provide easy access for placing and removing prints. This rack

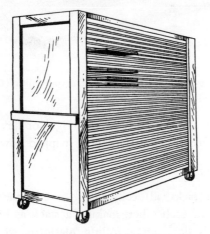

FIG. 24. Fixed shelf drying rack unit on casters.

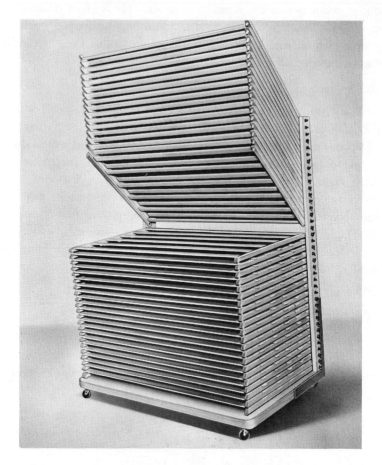

FIG. 25. One of several types of drop shelf drying units. (*Courtesy Cincinnati Screen Process Supplies, Inc.*)

is designed for all types of material, rigid or flexible. Each shelf stays in the lifted position until it is snapped down (Figure 25).

Loose Rack on a Truck

These loose racks, all constructed exactly the same size, are placed on top of each other, making a stack as high as practical. The stacking is done on a rolling platform, so that the entire

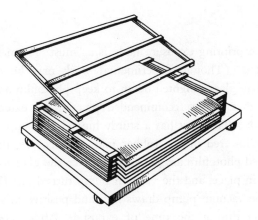

FIG. 26. Loose racks on dolly-stacking arrangement.

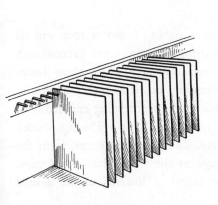

FIG. 27. Side-strip stacking arrangement for amateur use.

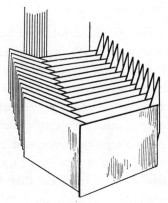

FIG. 28. Post support system for upright stacking of cards in an interlocking arrangement.

unit is mobile. This type of rack may be used for flexible or rigid material (Figure 26).

Figures 27 and 28 show suggestions for various improvisations of interest mostly as a matter of expediency for the amateur and small shop operator.

PHOTOGRAPHIC EQUIPMENT

Vacuum Table

A vacuum printing exposure table is a "must" for making good photo stencils. (Though experimental work may be done with sheets of plate glass weighted down to keep photofilm and positive in contact, that is not recommended practice for extended commercial work.) This unit has a sturdy hinged glass top which can be lifted or lowered over a rubber mat. In exposure, the positive and sensitized photofilm are placed in contact, the glass top lowered and locked in place, and the vacuum pump turned on. The suction action of the vacuum pump draws film and positive in strong uniform contact during the time of exposure. After exposure, the vacuum switch is turned off, allowing for the separation of the film and positive.

Arc Lights

Though No. 2 fotoflood bulbs in banks of two or four will do an acceptable job in illumination for exposure, most professionals prefer carbon arc lamps. The high amperage which these lamps develop at the carbon assures intensely brilliant, highly actinic illumination over the entire surface of the work being exposed. The Miller-Trojan arc lamp shown in Figure 29 is a 35-amp. model. It is a transformer operated lamp, using only 20 amps. from the line, though it develops 35 amps. at the arc. It has a telescopic stand so that the light may be raised or lowered to the desired height.

Printing-Exposure Combination Unit

This type of unit combines in a self-contained compact cabinet, an arc lamp and vacuum printing table, timer, etc. It is commercially marketed as the "Flip-Top" unit because the top, which is the vacuum printing section, flips or pivots inward to face the built-in carbon arc light below. After exposure, the top is flipped up again

FIG. 29. 35-amp model arc lamp. (*Courtesy Miller-Trojan Co.*)

and the exposed film is released ready for the developer. There are three steps to the flip-top unit shown here: (1) load (2) flip (3) expose (Figure 30).

Cameras

With the widespread use of photographic screens, photographic setup in modern shops includes a camera for making positives. Heretofore, it had been the general practice of most shops to get positives prepared "outside"; that is, by photoengravers who service the graphic art trade. Camera units vary tremendously in price, depending upon construction, lens, register controls and size of plate holders. Space does not permit here to show more than one which strikes an average in cost and versatility.

Fig. 30. Nu Arc "Flip-Top" vacuum exposure table with self contained arc lights. (*Courtesy Nu Arc Co.*)

The Miller-Trojan Model DC Process Camera in Figure 31 features a Wollensek Apochromatic lens calibrated with focusing tapes; two or four 1500-watt exposing lamps, a vacuum back operated by a ¼ h.p. pump, a glass-covered, rubber-cushioned copy board and easily operated controls. There are three sizes available to accommodate 11″ by 14″, 16″ by 20″, and 24″ square negatives.

FIG. 31. Miller-Trojan Process camera. (*Courtesy Miller-Trojan Co.*)

Miscellaneous Photographic Equipment

Other photo equipment includes an assortment of stainless steel or porcelain lined developing trays, spray hose, electric fan, etc; also a good quality thermostatic water mixer. This is used to maintain water at a pre-set controlled temperature. Equipment may be elaborated to include a stainless steel photo processing sink, humidifier and air conditioning and other modern photo darkroom facilities.

MISCELLANEOUS ACCESSORIES

Proof Horse

This is a mobile unit consisting of a wooden horse, on wheels, which carries a dispenser for a roll of newsprint paper. This is a facility, easily constructed and extremely useful for proofs. Rolls of newsprint come in 30″, 36″, 40″ and larger sizes, and provide an inexpensive and excellent surface for pretesting before production.

Mobile Tool Table

"Anybody here seen a hammer?" echoing throughout the shop is an indication of poor management in the maintenance of tools. A small table on casters should be equipped with compartments for an assortment of nails, screws, hinges, hammer, screwdriver, and other essential small tools needed for make-ready. The casters provide easy mobility so that the table can be wheeled where it is needed.

Make-ready Table

This, like the tool table, should be mobile and compartmentalized to include a can of fill-in lacquer, touch-up brushes, wiping cloth, adhering and washing thinner and other essentials needed for the adhering or washing of screens.

ART AND STENCIL CUTTING TOOLS

Art Tools

These would include a good mechanical instrument set, metal T-squares of various lengths, triangles, metal rules, an assortment of pencils, lettering brushes and pens, pencil sharpener, rubber cement dispenser, etc. This array of tools will reflect the nature and extent of all art work done on the premises.

Stencil Cutting Tools

While the lettering artist generally requires a sizeable assortment of brushes, the stencil cutter requires only a few stencil knives in his collection of work tools. One small-bladed stencil knife will cut large lettering or small, large designs or small. There are, however, several types of knives used.

The fixed-blade stencil knife shown in Figure 32 is nothing more than a small narrow blade, cut diagonally, fixed to a handle which

FIG. 32. Standard fixed-blade film stencil knife.

may be of wood, metal or plastic. The best blades are made of tempered surgical steel to retain a lasting cutting edge. This knife is also obtainable with interchangeable blade arrangements.

The swivel-blade knife shown in Figure 33 is a favorite among

FIG. 33. Ulano swivel knife with free-wheeling blade.

many stencil cutters, though it is at first rather difficult to control. The blade, small and triangular shaped, is made to rotate freely in a swivel action so that it takes the natural curves of the outline it traces. The handle is held firmly, it is not rotated. Only the blade rotates. However, the blade may, when desired, be fixed into position by a twist of a clutch. This instrument costs considerably more than the simple fixed blade knife, but it is a life-long precision tool made of fine surgical steel and requires little sharpening.

The double-line cutter is a double-bladed device, with a set screw adjustment which separates or closes the parallel blades, somewhat

FIG. 34. Double-line cutter with adjustable parallel blade spread.

similar in action to a ruling pen. It cuts two parallel lines simultaneously and may be adjusted in width. Its chief use is for cutting straight lines of even thickness for graph chart work and similar mechanical ruling (Figure 34).

Other double-line cutting tools are available with interchangeable parallel blade units in several fixed line thicknesses. Figure 35 illustrates such a type.

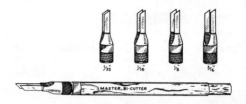

FIG. 35. Double-line cutter with interchangeable heads.

Compasses

There are several types. The bow compass shown in Figure 36 has an adjustable radius span, locked by a center wheel. One side of the fork carries a fine needle point which serves as the rotating center. The other side has an interchangeable lead pencil and cutting blade clutch holder. Special blades are available for such circle

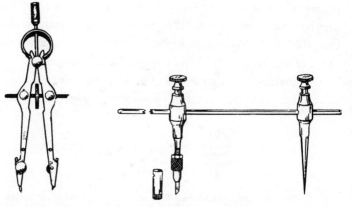

FIG. 36. Small bow compass with cutting blade attachment.

FIG. 37. Large beam compass with blade attachment for cutting circles.

cutters. Bow compasses come in two main sizes, a small one with a span of 4" diameter and a larger type with a 9" diameter. These instruments are also available with the adjusting screw on the outside, at one side of the fork. This is not as accurate as the center wheel type because of the tendency of both sides of the fork to flex. In the better type of instrument, the wheel is in the center. This locks the span so both sides cannot flex inadvertently.

For cutting very large circles a beam compass like the one shown in Figure 37 is used. This consists of a long metal rod with two movable units, one containing the center needle, the other holding a blade. By set screw arrangements, the span between the two can be locked. Beam compasses are also obtainable in miniature size; these operate on the same principle, but are designed for small circles (Figure 38).

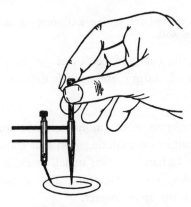

FIG. 38. Small beam compass.

Sharpening Stones

With proper use, the stencil blade will require very little sharpening. However, since the blade must be kept in a "click" sharp condition, some occasional sharpening is necessary. A small Arkansas stone is recommended. This is a smooth, hard stone which will, when the blade is passed over it several times, restore the cutting edge. Actually the blade should be delicately honed rather than vigorously sharpened. Arkansas stones come in small size units, 3" x 1" x ¼" and smaller.

"Cut-and-Peel" Knives

For cutting line and contour designs where a free stroke is permissible, the instrument shown in Figure 39 may be useful. This

FIG. 39. Special small tool for cutting and stripping in a single operation, useful in parallel line work.

type of stencil knife cuts and peels out the film in one stroke. It comes in a series of cutting sizes to suit different line thicknesses.

Burning Tool

This is the hobbyists' conventional electric wood-burning tool. It is virtually a miniature soldering iron and comes in a variety of different size tips. In hand-cut film stencil work, it is used for burning dots or stippling on lacquer film. The heated tip of the tool melts the film in spots upon contact.

Cutting Lamps

Though well engineered and expensive swivel-type fluorescent lamps are popular among artists and designers, they are not as good for the film cutter's needs as are the inexpensive gooseneck lamps that one can purchase in any hardware store. Fluorescent light, diffused as it is in a bar or long tube, does not concentrate the light in a small focal beam. The gooseneck light, with incandescent bulb shaded by a hood, directs the illumination on the film and is easily adjusted to spotlight the reflection of the trace-cut areas.

Enlarging Glasses

A film cutter's eyesight must be keen to enable him to cut very small type matter and design. For work of unusually fine detail,

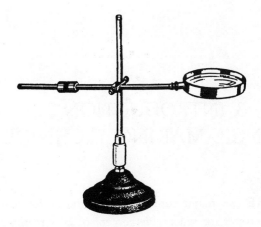

FIG. 40. Enlarging glass on stand for cutting fine detail.

several types of enlarging aids may be used. Figure 40 shows a flexible neck stand with magnifying glass.

A binocular eye loop which may be worn on the forehead in the manner of an eye shade, is often more practical than the stand magnifier. It fits comfortably, allowing free use of both hands and greater mobility.

Other tools, as has been said, would include the usual equipment for an art studio: metal rules, T-square, celluloid triangles, Scotch tape dispenser, etc.

3. INTRODUCTION TO
STENCIL MAKING TECHNIQUES

THERE ARE two major commercial techniques for making stencils which account for ninety-five percent of all screen work. These are the hand-cut film stencil technique and the photographic technique. In addition, there are minor techniques: the tusche method, popular for fine art print making, the block-out method and the cut-paper stencil methods. The basic principle of the stencil process can perhaps best be explained by referring to the simplest of these methods, the block-out method. This, then, will be the first method described, not because it is commercially important but because it will make the basic principle of the stencil easier for the beginner to understand.

LIQUID BLOCK-OUT METHODS

The screen fabric used in process work is composed of finely woven mesh which is porous in nature. If loose-flowing paint were poured within the frame on which the silk is stretched, the paint would slowly seep through. To make the flow-through faster and more even, a rubber squeegee is used.

A stencil can be formed by merely blocking or masking out part of the open mesh. The parts masked out would become impervious to the paint. The parts left open would permit flow-through. It is the various substances used to mask out the screen that differentiate one stencil making technique from another. In the liquid block-out method, the medium may be lacquer, shellac, or glue. Each of

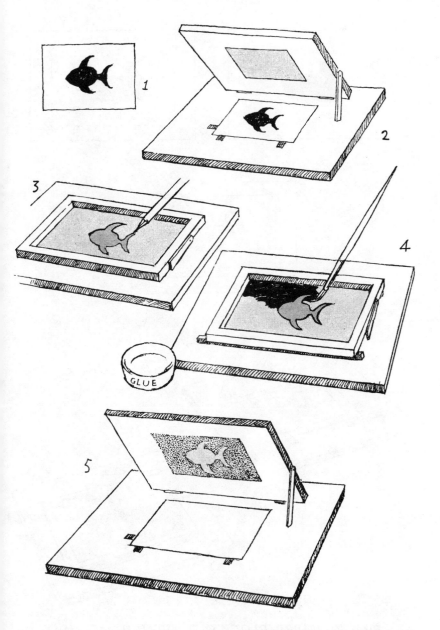

FIG. 41. LIQUID BLOCK-OUT STENCIL METHOD

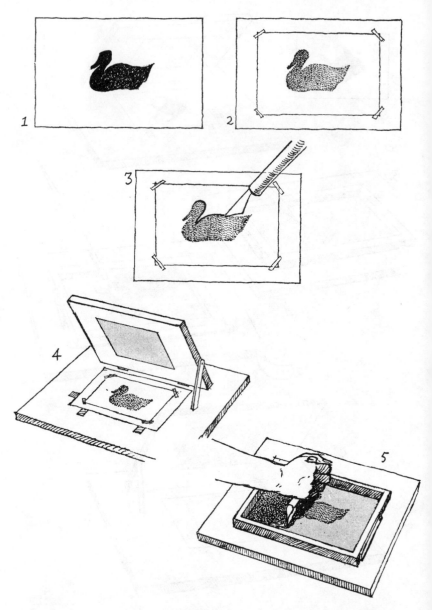

FIG. 42. PAPER BLOCK-OUT STENCIL METHOD

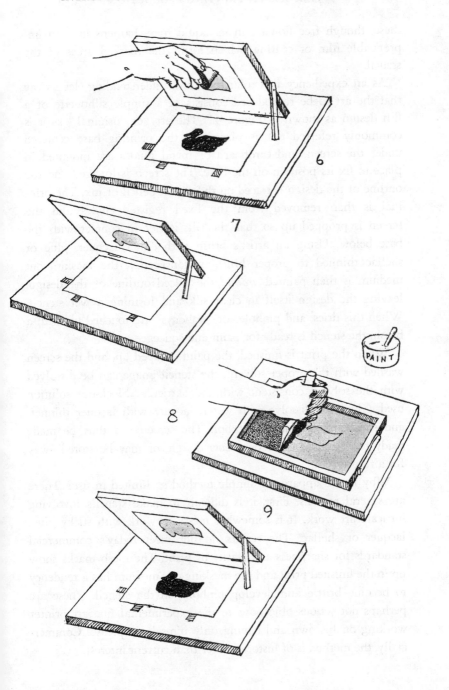

these, though free flowing in its liquid state, hardens into an impregnable film or coating, which forms the masked areas of the stencil.

As an expediency in explanation and understanding, let us say that the art to be reproduced consists of a simple silhouette of a fish design as shown in Figure 41. The art (or "original," as it is commonly referred to) is placed on the printing base centered under the screen, and cardboard or metal guides are mounted in place to fix its position on the base. The screen is lowered and the outline of the design is traced on the silk in pencil or ink. The original is then removed from the fixed register guides and the screen is propped up so that the silk is not in contact with the base below. Using an artist's brush with either lacquer, glue or shellac thinned to proper brushing consistency, the masking-out medium is then painted *around* the traced outline of the design, leaving the design itself in clear silk and forming a wet stencil. When this dries, and pinholes or "holidays" are touched up with a brush, the stencil is ready for paint and squeegee.

When the print is finished, the paint scooped up, and the screen washed with the proper solvent, the stencil image can be dissolved with the solvent consistent with the particular block-out solution used. Glue will dissolve with water, lacquer with lacquer thinner, and shellac is soluble in alcohol. The screen can thus be made ready for the next color or a new design, or may be stored away for a future rerun.

Why is this apparently simple method so limited in use? There are several reasons. First, it is difficult to make stencils involving intricate art work. It is somewhat messy to work with sticky glue, lacquer or shellac. The results do not meet today's commercial standards for sharpness and clarity of print. The mesh marks show up in the finished print and the masking-out medium has a tendency to become brittle and develop pinholes in the stencil. These are perhaps not serious objections to the experimental fine art printer working on his own and having only himself to please. Commercially, the method is of historic rather than current interest.

PAPER BLOCK-OUT METHOD

The principle is the same, except that thin paper is used as a masking medium (Figure 42).

To refer to our experimental fish design described above, the original is placed in the fixed guide, the same as before. The screen is propped up so that the screen frame is perpendicular to the base. A thin sheet of ordinary bond or translucent sign paper is temporarily taped over the art work on the base. Using a well-sharpened stencil knife, the outline of the fish is trace-cut. The cut area is not lifted out; it is left in place. The tape is carefully removed without shifting the cut paper. The screen is then lowered over the paper and color is poured into the screen ready for printing. After several side-to-side squeegee movements across the screen, the screen is carefully lifted. It will be found that the paint has, because of its viscous consistency, acted as an adhering agent for the paper, and has lifted the stencil, with the entire paper still clinging to the underside of the silk. The silhouette of the fish (the part to be printed) is now carefully lifted off the silk. This opens the stencil. The printing operation commences at this point. When the job of printing is done, the paint is removed as usual, the screen washed and the mask of paper peeled off the silk. It will come off without resistance, once the paint is no longer there to hold it.

The paper stencil method has excellent potentials for the commercial printer specializing in large posters in limited editions. The stencil can last for several hundred sharp prints before the paper mask wears down. The prints of a paper stencil are characterized by knife-cut sharp edges with a slightly raised surface due to the thickness of the paper mask.

The paper stencil cannot be re-used or saved for a rerun. It is a one-shot affair, good for supermarket signs and 24-sheet posters and the like.

THE TUSCHE-GLUE STENCIL METHOD

By far, the tusche method is the most popular among serigraphic artists and print makers. The reasons are many, among which are these: it invites experimentation with dry brush and textural crayon effects; the stencil image is clearly visible on the screen before the print is made; it permits the artist to improvise as he makes his stencils.

Commercially, limitations to the tusche method consist mainly in the fact that the print edges are rather rough, pinholes are likely to develop in the screen and an unusual degree of skill is necessary to make stencils involving small lettering or delicate designs.

Briefly stated, here are the steps in the making of a tusche-glue resist stencil. For the sake of simplification, let us assume that the original to be reproduced is a simple design like the sailboat shown in Figure 43.

The original is set in the guides on the base in the manner described previously. With the screen lowered over the art, the design is trace-painted right on the screen with brush and a liquid resist medium known as tusche. This has the unique property of being soluble in water, kerosene or turpentine. Tusche is a black liquid of the consistency of paint and has a somewhat wax-like feel to it, but brushes easily. An exact facsimile of the art is "tusched" over the screen, giving a preview of the finished print, as it might look in black. When the tusche painting sets (it never really dries hard), the entire screen is covered with a solution of water mixed with glue in about equal proportions. This glue mixture is best applied by scraping it smoothly and evenly once or twice across the upper surface of the screen (the side on which the tusche is applied) with the screen removed from its hinges and propped up on two sticks. Within half an hour or so, the glue dries, forming a smooth hard film with the tusche area trapped underneath. Then both sides of the screen are soaked with kerosene and vigorously scrubbed down with a kerosene-soaked rag, with special attention paid to the underside of the silk beneath the tusched design.

Here is what happens. Kerosene is a solvent of tusche, but not of glue. Hence the kerosene bath attacks the tusche only and loosens its hold on the screen. The glue crust on top of it, losing its anchorage, floats off, having nothing to hold onto. The result is a stencil formed by a glue film with openings of clear silk which

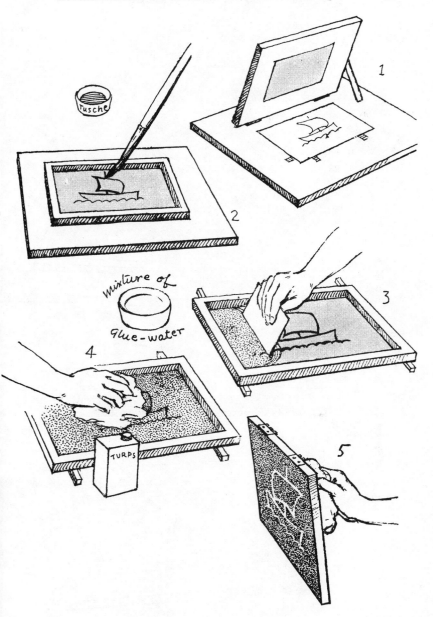

FIG. 43. TUSCHE-GLUE RESIST STENCIL METHOD
(Unsized Screen)

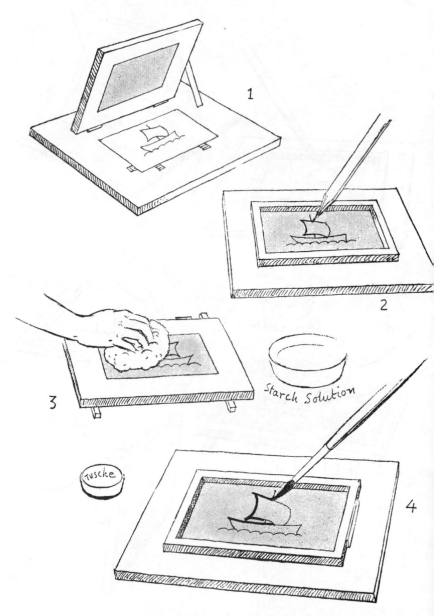

FIG. 44. TUSCHE-GLUE RESIST STENCIL METHOD
(Sized Screen)

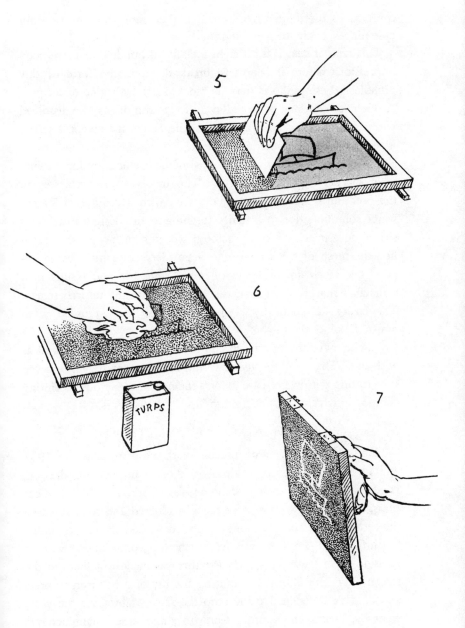

conform to the design. The screen is then reset into the printing base hinges, ready for paint and squeegee.

This type of stencil is all right for several hundred or more good impressions before it begins to break down in the form of tiny pinholes. These pinholes may be blocked out with glue or lacquer. A tusche screen may be stored away for re-run or may be dissolved with a generous wash of warm water. Cleaned of the glue, the screen is ready to accept another assignment.

There is another variation of this method which produces somewhat sharper edges (Figure 44). This involves one extra step in the procedure, namely sizing the screen with a coating of starch-water solution prior to actually tusching-in the design areas. This sizing, once it dries, forms a smooth working surface as the starch fills the mesh of the screen with a powdery covering. Tusche applied over such an area goes on more smoothly and results in a somewhat sharper print than that possible with the unsized screen. The sizing automatically comes off during the kerosene wash which dissolves the tusche.

Tusche may also be used in combination with lacquer as well as with glue. The resulting stencil would be a lacquer stencil reserved for printing with water-base colors, enamels and any other printing compound which does not contain lacquer ingredients.

THE HAND-CUT FILM METHOD

Hand-cut film for screen process work was introduced in 1931 and its later technical development, though not its introduction, is generally credited to Joe Ulano of New York. The first hand-cut films, crude as they were, were quickly adopted and soon replaced the earlier tusche and block-out methods described above. Originally, a film, called Profilm, was of a shellac composition, with a glassine paper back. This early Profilm was made to adhere to the screen only with difficulty, requiring the use of a hot iron to press and dissolve the stencil tissue onto the screen fabric. As the years went by, Ulano, the Profilm Company, and other manufacturers continued to improve their films, and developed many different types for varied uses. Today, lacquer films are sold under such trade names as Nufilm, Blufilm, Ulano film, Profilm, etc.

For the sake of clarity in describing the hand-cut film stencil method, let us say that the art work we want reproduced consists of the single word "Yale." We will carry on the description with that arbitrary assumption (Figure 45).

The original art may be done in pencil, paint or ink. We are not concerned with the technique in which the art is rendered. With art for hand-cut screens, unlike that required for photographic stencils, we are concerned only with outlines or boundaries of the design.

The film (lacquer side up) is taped securely over the art. Because the film is transparent, the art below it is clearly visible underneath. With the film in place, we are ready for cutting the design. The cutting tool is a small-bladed stylus of which there are several types on the market (as shown on page 29). The outlines of the design are trace-cut lightly, care being taken not to apply so much pressure on the stencil knife as to penetrate the thin backing sheet underneath. It takes practice to "feel" and control the knife pressure. To an experienced stencil cutter, this is second nature. All cuts are made to cross at intersections to be sure that the outline is completely cut. The "cross cuts" do not show in the finished print, though they can be seen on the stencil film. When the complete design is thus trace-cut, the parts within the cut areas are lifted and the upper skin of lacquer is stripped off, leaving the exposed area of backing sheet showing through. The art, with the film still intact, is next placed in the register guides, previously fixed to the base. The screen is then lowered and we are ready for the succeeding step which is the adhesion of the film.

With the silk lowered over the film and in close contact with it, the upper surface of the screen is rubbed over once or twice with a soft rag saturated with adhering thinner. The "adherer," which is really a lacquer solvent, slightly softens the upper part of the film (which is a lacquer composition) and makes it cling to the silk. This solvent application is immediately followed with a dry

FIG. 45. HAND-CUT FILM STENCIL METHOD

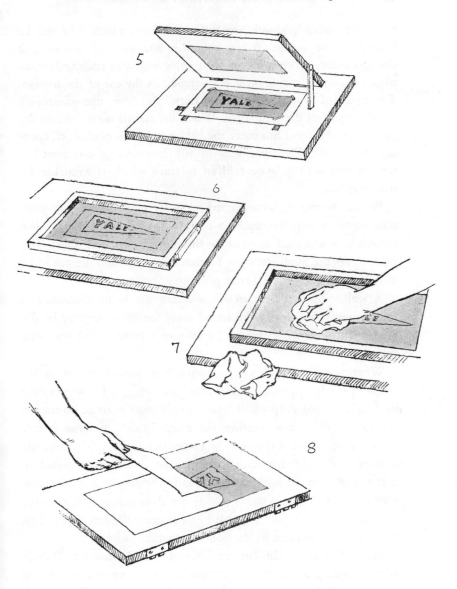

rag rub to quickly absorb any trace of solvent which may still be lodged in the screen. When the film has adhered properly, it changes color, and the evenness of color indicates uniformly complete adhesion. Caution must be exercised in the use of the thinner. Too much of it may dissolve or "burn" the film, thus destroying the sharpness of the film edges. When the stencil is completely dry (a matter of several minutes) the backing sheet is peeled off, opening the stencil. The open area of silk surrounding the stencil is then coated with a lacquer fill-in mixture which is available for that purpose.

Before the stencil is considered ready for use, it should be given a kerosene or naphtha wash to remove any traces of the residual cement that was used to combine the film and backing sheet. This wash clears the mesh, removes foreign matter around the cut edges of the stencil and assures better printing impressions.

A well made hand-cut stencil will last for many thousands of sharp impressions. It may be stored away for re-use or may be dissolved with a generous wash of a lacquer solvent called removing thinner.

Whereas the procedure is comparatively simple and is in the realm of easily acquirable knowledge, the cutting of a stencil calls for long acquired skill—skill attained only after years of on-the-job experience. Of course, cutting the word "Yale" in large letters, as shown in Figure 45, would be comparatively simple. There are craftsmen who through long years of experience have acquired an uncanny skill in cutting the finest detail. The test of a good craftsman is in his skill as a cutter of fine detail in design and lettering. For this skill, he is well rewarded and is generally one of the best paid craftsmen in most screen printing establishments.

The technique of film cutting deserves special attention. Though merely reading about it will obviously not automatically develop the skill, still it may serve as a suggested course of study for those whose special interest may be directed to this phase of stencil making. Some trade schools offer an extensive course in this highly skilled craft.

FILM CUTTING EXERCISES

Skill in cutting is developed only through persistent practice. It takes years, not months or weeks, to become an expert in the craft. A good film cutter is more than a mere tracer. He must have a knowledge of letter construction, spacing, color separation, etc. Indeed, one of the chief reasons for using a hand-cut stencil rather than doing the job by means of photographic stencils, is that quite frequently the original art that one has to work from is hardly more than a rough "comp" or a mere pencil sketch. It is the job of the cutter to correct, improvise and improve the art, in the process of cutting the stencil. If he has the background of a letterer, he is not considered in the category of a mere tracer, and his value in the stencil department is much greater. The following exercises, typical of many practice drills developed in courses in film cutting taught in schools, may have some value in self-instruction and may serve as the basis for other exercises that you can develop yourself.

Exercise 1 (Figure 46)

On a 11" x 14" white cardboard, draw in pencil outline several

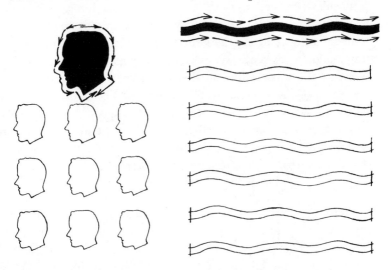

FIG. 46. Film cutting drill #1. Silhouettes.

FIG. 47. Film cutting drill #2. Waves.

profiles or silhouette outlines of a head about 2″ high. This comprises your "art." In cutting the film for this exercise, start on the crown of the head and, going down counter-clockwise, trace-cut the contour in one continuous movement, until you reach halfway up the underside of the neckline. Then starting on the crown again, and overlapping by about ⅛″ the previous starting line, trace-cut the contour going down the back of the head in a clockwise direction, until you meet and overlap the previous finish line. When this is done, insert the tip of the blade at the lower part of the silhouette and gently lift the entire film silhouette, attempting to strip it in one piece. It does not really matter if the film is peeled in sections, but it is good practice and a greater time saver to get into the habit of using a minimum of movements. Continue with many plates of this exercise, making each plate progressively more difficult by making the heads smaller in size.

Exercise 2 (Figure 47)

Prepare an outline drawing of a series of wavy snake lines, similar to that shown here. Holding the knife in an almost perpendicular position, trace-cut in one continuous left-to-right movement the upper edge of the wavy line, going from terminal to terminal without lifting the knife until the end of the line. Repeat this motion with the lower edge, again going from left to right. Now cut the vertical line on the right side, then on the left side, always as a down stroke from north to south. Be sure that you overcut or cross your lines as a precaution against leaving uncut gaps. These overcuts, though they show up in the film, do not show in the finished print. Now, starting at either end, lift a corner of the film and strip the entire wave as one section of film.

Exercise 3 (Figure 48)

Prepare a chart showing a series of egg-shaped ovals. Starting at the "crown" or crest of the egg, and going counter-clockwise, cut with a continuous movement until the base of the egg is reached. Next, start at the crown once more and overlap into the groove which marked the previous starting point, trace-cut the right-hand side of the egg, until the previous finishing terminal has been

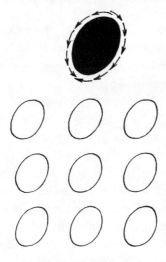

FIG. 48. Film cutting drill #3. Ovals.

reached, and overlap about ⅛″ into that. This overlap assures complete coverage.

These and similar exercises will help you gain proficiency in freehand cutting. Other systematic exercises may be developed for cutting straight lines, both freehand and with a straight edge; mechanically round circles, to gain proficiency in using the knife compass; and lettering of diminishing size, to develop close attention to fine detail.

TEN HINTS IN CUTTING FILM

1. Be sure to illuminate the work with a movable direct light. Ordinary ceiling overhead lights, no matter how apparently bright, are not sufficient. An adjustable gooseneck-type flexible lamp is best for the job.

2. Be sure that your hands are free from grease or perspiration. Grease smudges transferred to the film may impair proper adhesion to the screen. Also be sure that the film is free from particles of dust or dirt, which may imbed themselves in the adhesion and cause a blemish in the screen.

3. The knife blade must be scalpel-sharp so that pressure will not have to be exerted in cutting. A dull blade forces you to apply

considerable pressure and consequently forms deep trenches in the backing sheet. This may offer a problem in the adhesion of the film.

4. Overcut and criss-cross all joining lines in the design. This practice assures complete "coverage" and facilitates stripping the film. The overcuts do not show in the print.

5. The stencil knife is a delicate instrument. Do not use it as a tack remover or general utility tool. It often takes considerable effort to restore the blade edge to its click-sharp condition, so treat the stencil knife carefully. It is your silent partner in your craft.

6. Get acquainted with the use of various cutting devices, such as the fixed-blade knife, the swivel knife, the double cutter for ruling uniform even parallel lines, the compass cutter for circles, the scraper for special crosshatch line effects, and the woodburning tool for melting stipple dots (see Figures 32 to 40).

7. Keep the film well covered, especially after it is stripped, to avoid dust or damage.

8. Examine your cut film closely for "mistakes," omissions, and presence of foreign matter, *before* adhesion of the film. To do so later means delay in printing and at best a badly repaired stencil job.

9. Pieces of cut film that have been inadvertently removed or have fallen away while cutting the stencil may be replaced in position with a touch of diluted rubber cement.

10. Mark each film distinctly as to the particular color it corresponds to on the art, and its position in the sequence of printing. In a multicolor job, it is often hard to tell which color is which by merely looking at apparently disjointed areas of the cut film. Register cross marks must appear on all films to assist in aligning the related colors.

SIX HINTS FOR ADHESION OF THE FILM

1. Be sure that the silk is properly prepared for adhesion. This means that whether the screen is new or has been previously used, it must be thoroughly washed with hot water and scrubbed with stiff brushes to remove all traces of size, grease, and fatty residues from paint, kerosene or varnish. If the screen is not properly pre-

pared, it will retard good and complete marriage between film and silk.

2. Check on the contact between silk and film. The greatest single cause of "burned" edges, aside from poor cutting, is poor contact during the adhesion. If the silk and film do not meet uniformly, the adhering solvent may collect in puddles as it reaches into the "pockets" or spaces between the silk and the film. The excess of solvent collected in these pockets will dissolve the edges of the film and result in a poor stencil.

3. Use only the solvent recommended by the manufacturer of the film. Film and solvent must be made for each other.

4. Use soft clean rags for the adhesion. A woolly absorbent cloth is preferred to a silky, non-absorbent kind. Rags which have been used before and have collected grease, grime or dirt will not do the job adequately.

5. Use an electric fan to blow on the screen during the adhesion of the film. A flow of air will help to evaporate the adhering thinner as quickly as possible before it has a chance to dissolve the film.

6. Allow the film to dry thoroughly before stripping the backing sheet. Stripping this too soon may pull along some edges and result in poor adhesion and consequently poor printing.

ADDITIONAL NOTES ON HAND-CUT FILM STENCILS

Lacquer film is composed of a very thin layer of lacquer temporarily laminated with a rubber cement solution to a transparent backing sheet. This backing sheet may be wax paper, acetate, or other transparent plastic material. The purpose of the backing sheet is to hold the stencil with its cut film elements until after the cut film has adhered to the screen, after which, the backing sheet having served its purpose, it is stripped away from the screen.

The early film tissue used in the industry was a material composed not of lacquer, but of shellac. This was known as Profilm and required the application and pressure of a heated flatiron to soften the lacquer to make it adhere to the screen. This procedure was rather involved and was gradually replaced by a lacquer type of film, introduced by the Nufilm Company. This improved film adhered easily and quickly with a lacquer solvent. Stencil films come in various colors, such as amber, green, blue, etc. The choice of a particular color is a matter of personal preference and bears no functional relationship to the color of the paint for which the stencil is intended.

There are two recent developments in films which are worthy of note:

1. Water-soluble films. Several film suppliers have individually developed hand-cut films which can adhere with water. This offers a number of advantages over the standard lacquer type film which requires lacquer solvent as an adhering fluid. Nufilm's Water Soluble hand-cut stencil film as well as Ulano's Aquafilm are primarily intended for use in screening vinyl inks, enamels, lacquers and other compounds which are unsuitable for lacquer film stencils. Though they are somewhat more expensive than lacquer films, there is an obvious saving in the cost of adhering since the adhering agent is water. Avoiding the use of lacquer and inflammable lacquer thinner removes a fire hazard, and thus makes the water-soluble film well suited for home or class use. One natural drawback to a water-soluble film stencil is that it cannot be used with water base paints or tempera colors.

2. Photo-masking film. This material, though widely used in the making of photographic stencils, is not confined to the silk screen industry only. Red or deep amber in color, this knife-cut film is laminated to a stable transparent plastic backing sheet. The red or amber colors are "light safe" so that when the film is used as a photographic transparency, the colored tissue serves as an opaquing mask for the exposure. This film offers many advantages over the hand-painted transparencies. Cutting and stripping are much faster operations than brush painting by hand. What is more, the results are better. The film is widely used now by photoengravers for hand-cut color separations for camera work.

4. INTRODUCTION TO
PHOTO STENCIL METHODS

ALTHOUGH tremendous strides in improving photo stencil methods have been made in the past decade, and yet greater improvements in photo techniques and products no doubt await us, it is safe to say that photo stencils will never completely replace hand-cut stencils. Why? Because the photo copy camera requires perfect and finished art work. The camera cannot correct poor spacing in lettering, shaky unfinished lines in art; it cannot make intelligent and artistic decisions or revisions in the art. With its objective and fixed eye, the camera reproduces what it sees. Hand-cut screens, on the other hand, can be made from a mere rough pencil sketch. The art is "finished," as it were, as the stencil is being cut. However, it is nonetheless a fact that more and more art is being prepared for the camera, and greater use of photography is being made by screen process as time goes on.

In this chapter, we will not attempt a definitive treatment of photographic techniques. There are at present several good books on the market devoted exclusively to photographic silk screen work. Among them are *Photographic Process Printing* by Albert Kosloff, and *Techniques in Photography for the Silk Screen Printer* by Robert O. Fossett. Suffice it here, in this general treatment of the process as a whole, to confine ourselves to the task of simplifying the techniques for the orientation of the reader new to the process.

The basic photographic principle is this: light passing through unobstructed to a chemically sensitized area, brings about a structural chemical change. The condition of openness or obstruction of the light is inherent in a photo transparency. The black opaque parts do not permit the light to pass through. The light passes through the clear areas only. When light hits the sensitized area, it hardens it. The parts shielded from the light dissolve in water.

BASIC METHODS

There are two main applications of the above principle to screen process. One is called the *direct* method, the other the *transfer* method.

Direct Method (Figure 49)

Here the screen is coated with a sensitized photographically active gelatinous solution which forms the structure of the stencil. Parts of it will dissolve, parts will not dissolve, in direct relation to the image on the transparency. What gelatin remains undissolved, in its hardened state, forms the stencil. Paint can be squeegeed through the openings, thus producing a facsimile print of the original art.

Transfer Method

Here the photographic principle of light as it affects a sensitized material is the same as in the direct method referred to before. The main difference between the two is that in the transfer method a gelatinous film sheet—not the screen itself—is sensitized. After exposing and developing, the film is transferred to the screen.

In the main, the transfer photo film consists of a laminated sheet, made up of two micro-thin tissues. The top side is a gelatin emulsion, the underside is a transparent backing sheet which acts as a support until the stencil has adhered to the screen. After that, having served its purpose, the backing sheet is peeled off, opening the stencil.

Transfer photo stencil films are sold under many different trade names, but they all involve the same principle. Although it is recommended that the reader experiment with the products of several manufacturers, it will simplify matters here to select at random a single manufacturer's product in order to avoid repetition or variations in instructions. The instructions given below are condensed from the instruction brochure issued by the McGraw

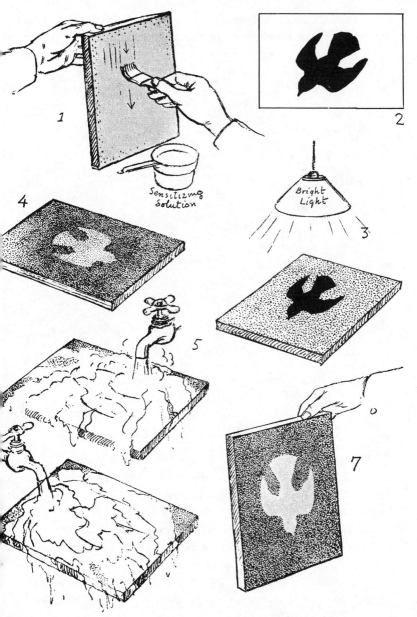

FIG. 49. PRINCIPLE OF THE DIRECT PHOTO STENCIL
METHOD

Colorgraphic Company, one of the prime suppliers of carbon tissue and other graphic art photographic materials.

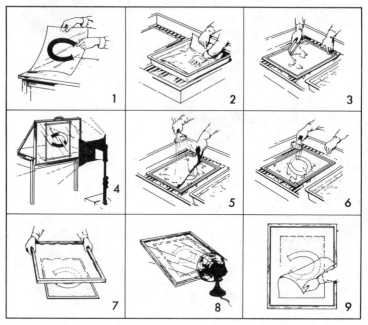

FIG. 50. Carbon tissue photo stencil method. (*Courtesy McGraw Colorgraphic Co.*)

THE CARBON TISSUE METHOD (Figure 50)

The carbon tissue method involves a double transfer of the stencil image. In the single transfer methods described previously, the stencil image of the gelatin is directly applied to the screen. In the carbon tissue, on the other hand, the gelatinous stencil image is first transferred onto a plastic backing surface and then *transferred* to the screen. It is perhaps because of this double jeopardy and additional opportunity for error that the carbon tissue method is not as widely used by silk screen processors with limited photographic experience, although the method is generally regarded as the one yielding the truest reproduction and the finest results.

The carbon tissue method derives its name from the fact that the gelatinous coating of the photographic paper is pigmented with a carbon black to make the stencil image visible.

In essence, production of a carbon tissue photo stencil involves the following steps:

1. Inspect the positive. As in all photo stencil methods, the positive must be carefully checked for opacity, presence of dirt, pinholes and other irregularities.

2. Sensitize the carbon tissue paper. Fill a clean tray to a depth of at least one inch, with a cool (below 68 degrees F.) 2 per cent solution of potassium dichromate. Cut a sheet of pigment paper a little larger than the positive, and a sheet of "mylar" plastic a little larger than the pigment paper. (The "mylar" sheet will later act as a temporary support for the pigment paper.) Immerse the pigment paper (emulsion side facing up) in the sensitizer and rock the tray slightly to get a free agitation of the sensitizer over the surface of the paper.

3. Mount on temporary support. Place the sheet of "mylar" support on a smooth flat surface. Wet the support thoroughly with sensitizer. Position the emulsion side of the pigment paper in contact with the support. To be sure of perfect contact between the emulsion and plastic support, squeegee lightly from the center toward the outer edges. This also helps to remove any air which may be trapped between the emulsion and the plastic. Wipe off excess sensitizer from the paper back, then turn the lamination of plastic and paper over and thoroughly dry the back of the plastic.

4. Expose. Position the positive and plastic-paper lamination in the print frame, with the emulsion side of the positive in contact with the plastic. With opaque paper or black tape, mask the edges of the pigment paper so that a ½″ margin all around will remain unexposed. Refer to the manufacturer's instruction sheet for exposure times. In addition, make several prior test shots to serve as a guide simulating actual conditions.

5. Remove paper backing. Position the exposed pigment paper-plastic sandwich, paper side up, on a piece of glass which drains into a sink. Flood the gelatin emulsion with hot water (110°–

120° F.) until it begins to ooze from the edges, then carefully strip up and discard the paper.

6. Wash out. Continue to run the hot water over the image on the support until all soluble gelatin is thoroughly dissolved and the water draining from the image is clear. Then chill with cold water.

7. Fasten to screen. Place the stencil on its temporary support, emulsion side up, on a heavy piece of masonite or similar flat material. This support should be a little larger than the stencil, but smaller than the screen frame. Place the screen, frame side up, in contact with the stencil. Press evenly and remove the excess moisture by blotting with newsprint paper or lintless blotters.

8. Dry the stencil. The screen may dry naturally or a fan may be used to hasten the drying.

9. Remove temporary support. When the stencil is thoroughly dry, the temporary support will strip from the stencil easily.

The difference between a good stencil and one that is inferior will in large measure depend upon many judgments which can come only through experience and trial and error.

ULANO WET-SHOT PHOTO FILM

This is a simple transfer method in wide use today. One of the distinct advantages of this film is that it may be exposed immediately after sensitizing. In some film stencil methods, the film, after being sensitized, must be stored and allowed to dry. The drying process is time-consuming and also provides an opportunity for dust to collect on the film. The procedure for making a Wet-Shot film stencil is comparatively simple and does not require extensive knowledge of photo science. Of course, judgment acquired through experience will make a decided difference in the finished result.

In essence, the steps are as follows:

The film is sensitized with an easily prepared bichromate sensitizer. It is then blotted and wiped dry, placed in a vacuum frame with a positive, exposed to a light source, washed out in warm water, and affixed to the screen. When dry, the backing sheet is removed. Detailed instructions for each step of the procedure follow.

Sensitizing

The materials for mixing the sensitizing solution are available from the dealer who sells the Wet-Shot film. Ammonium bichromate is the chemical used. Generally speaking, a low bichromate concentration produces a hard film and a high bichromate solution produces a softer film. This fact is important, because by means of this control coupled with varying lengths of exposure, you can produce the type of film needed for specific jobs. The best film is one that has a hard bottom and a tacky top since it stands up best on long runs and yields the sharpest prints.

To prepare the sensitizing solution, dissolve 1 oz. (28 grams) of ammonium bichromate in 16 fluid ounces of distilled water. This is a stock solution and should be stored in a brown bottle in a cool place. This stock solution is mixed with ethyl or isopropyl alcohol. The purpose of the alcohol in the sensitizer is to prevent the film from melting during exposure. It is important to point out that bichromate solution which gets warm or is kept in bright light is subject to deterioration. Kept cool and in a brown bottle, the solution will last for months.

A word of caution about bichromate. This is a poison which may have a deteriorative effect on the skin of those who suffer from dermatological allergies. It is good professional practice to use rubber gloves in handling this chemical.

For making a working solution of sensitizer, mix one part of stock solution to three parts of alcohol.

There are three ways of applying the solution to the film:

1. *Brush method.* Lightly tape or tack Wet-Shot film (film side up) to a wooden board. Using a good grade of camel's hair brush, apply a generous, even coat of sensitizer in criss-cross fashion. Be sure the entire surface of the film is covered and well saturated, as it is necessary that the sensitizing solution actually penetrate the surface of the film.

Having previously prepared a piece of kraft paper (the kind

used for brown wrapping paper) at least one inch bigger all around than the film itself, remove the sensitized film from the board and place the kraft paper on top of the wet film. Then apply a soaking wet coat of sensitizer right over the kraft paper. Now, flip the kraft paper over so that the coated paper is against the wet film, applying a generous coat to the back side of the kraft paper. When that is done, remove the excess sensitizer from the kraft paper, using absorbent newsprint as a blotting agent. That done, turn the Wet-Shot and kraft paper over and clean the plastic side of the Wet-Shot film with a rag to remove the sensitizer.

2. *Roller method.* Instructions are the same, except that instead of using a camel's hair brush to spread the sensitizer over the film, use a soft lint-free cloth paint roller to distribute the solution. A good grade of standard paint roller obtainable in most hardware or paint stores is fine for the purpose.

3. *Tray method.* This is considered by many to be the most efficient way to apply the sensitizer. Use a clean porcelain or stainless steel tray, large enough to accommodate the size of film to be sensitized. Pour a sufficient working solution into the tray. In it place a sheet of kraft paper about one inch bigger all around than the film. The soaked paper will slowly sink to the bottom of the tray where it is left until you are ready for combining. Now place the film, emulsion side up, in the tray, leaving it there for about 90 seconds. Next, turn the film over, emulsion side facing down, so that it comes in contact with the kraft paper. Remove both together from the tray. On a pile of newsprint paper, smoothly surfaced, place the combination of kraft paper and film (plastic side up). Using a soft damp rag clean the sensitizer off the plastic side of the film, removing excess or dripping solution. The film is now ready for the vacuum table and the next step, which is exposing.

Exposing

There are various kinds of lights and exposure units produced by photo equipment firms which service the graphic arts. Personal preference will favor one over the other types, but in general the principle of exposure is the same. Exposure time cannot be exactly fixed, as that will vary with a number of factors. These are: the nature of the positive, the distance of light from the point of exposure, the kind of light, the nature of the art work, etc. As a guide only, it may serve some purpose to say that a 90 second exposure, 36 inches from a 35 amp. single arc would be right for "average" conditions. Time of exposure is a matter of seasoned judgment and even the best of photographic stencil makers occasionally misjudge. A good policy is to make a test before proceeding with an important job. In general, it is good to remember that underexposure will produce a thin, weak film. Overexposure will produce a heavy film. If the film is thin, it will yield fine reproduction qualities but the chances are that the stencil will not last long, may develop pinholes or may even partly wash away in developing. A film which has been overexposed will suffer because of loss of detail.

The plate glass of the contact table must be thoroughly clean, free from dust or fingerprints. Every impurity directly over the film will result in a corresponding imperfection in the photo stencil. The positive transparency, too, which is placed in contact with the film must be clean, pinhole-free and flat.

Note: The procedure for the setup for exposure is as follows: Keep a sheet of plastic in the vacuum frame to keep the protective blanket clean. Place a small pile of newsprint on the plastic. Put the film-kraft paper sandwich (kraft paper side up) on the newsprint. Put the positive with the emulsion side in contact with the plastic side of the film, and cover the whole assembly with another sheet of clear plastic. This last sheet will keep the plate glass on the vacuum free from stains and dampness. Lower the frame, start the vacuum, set the timer, and switch on the exposure light.

Washing Out

After exposure, place the film, kraft paper cover up, in a tray filled with water heated to a temperature of about 110° F. In about 15 to 20 seconds you may slip the kraft paper off the film; it should come off without resistance. Peel it off and continue washing until the design appears as a visible image on the film. You may further help the wash out with a gentle spray. The image should finally appear clear and sharp and free from any residual gelatinous matter.

Note: The behavior of the kraft paper indicates the accuracy of the exposure time. If overexposed, the paper cover will either not release at all, or come off with difficulty.

Adhering

Remove the film from the tray and place it gelatin side up on a smooth pack of newsprint sheets to remove water from the backing sheet. Next, place the film in proper register on the printing table. To assure accuracy of position or register, the film may be placed directly over a print of the previous color or over the original art work, care of course being taken to protect the art work with a sheet of acetate or other protective transparent tissue. With the film thus secured in position, the screen is carefully lowered over the film so that screen and wet film below are now in perfect contact. Now, using flat sheets of newsprint as a drying-blotting medium, dry-blot the screen evenly and firmly over the film. As one sheet of newsprint takes on the moisture, discard it and take another sheet. Continue replacing the sheets until all moisture is absorbed. When you now lift the screen you will find that the film is adhered securely to the screen. Now raise the screen all the way over so that it lies flat (adhered film side up), or disengage the screen from hinges by removing pins, and place the screen upside down on a flat table and prepare for the next steps, which are: (1) filling in the screen to close the open meshes surrounding the film, and (2) stripping the backing sheet.

1. *Filling in the screen.* Use a water soluble fill-in solution as a block-out material. This is obtainable from most silk screen suppliers. Pour this at one end of the screen (still upside down) right over the entire screen, backing sheet and all. Use a smooth straight-edged piece of stiff cardboard as a squeegee for fast and even application. (Do not be alarmed, nothing can happen to the film, because you are applying the fill-in solution over the backing sheet which protects it.) Place the screen under a fan to dry. After the

screen is dry, apply a second coat of the fill-in material and allow the screen to dry thoroughly.

2. *Stripping the backing sheet.* After the film is dry, it changes color somewhat, a sign that the backing sheet is ready to be peeled off. If the backing sheet does not come off easily, it is a sign that the film is not completely dry. The backing sheet, when the film is thoroughly dry, will peel off easily in one sheet if you merely raise one corner and lift the entire sheet away.

When the backing sheet is removed, wash the film with naphtha, benzine, kerosene, or turpentine. This wash removes any cement deposit which may have clung to the film after the backing sheet is removed. Now, hold the screen up to the light and touch up any pinholes in the stencil.

Note: The quality of a photo stencil depends upon many factors: the various steps in the procedure outlined above, the condition of the photo positive, scientific cleanliness in handling materials, etc. An important prerequisite, in a class by itself, is the type and condition of the screen fabric which is to receive the photofilm. Because this aspect is so important, and applies to all types of photo stencil methods, it will be given special emphasis in the chapter on screen fabrics. Note that no mention of a darkroom was made in these instructions. For this method, the operator may work in ordinary light but away from strong, direct light. The film does not become sensitive to light until it receives the sensitizer solution. Even then, it does not respond quickly to normal light and may be momentarily handled in average room light until it is placed on the exposure table.

PRESENSITIZED PHOTO STENCIL METHOD

On the market today, there are a number of presensitized photo films. These free the operator from one step in the procedure in making photo stencils, namely, sensitizing the film before exposure. There are other advantages which merit consideration. The Ulano "Hi-Fi" presensitized photo film, one of several trade brands of this type of film, has the following features:

1. It is ready for immediate use.

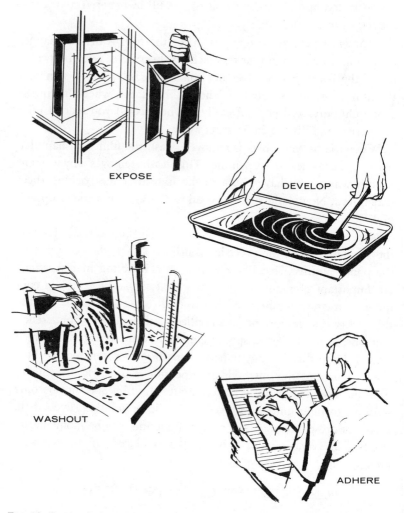

FIG. 51. Four major steps in the presensitized photo stencil procedure. (*Courtesy Ulano Products Co.*)

2. It has a long shelf life.

3. It is recommended for long runs because the film is thick and durable.

4. It has a special plastic backing which insures controlled register.

5. It has good adhesive qualities to wire, silk, nylon, and other screen materials.

6. It does not require a darkroom.

The steps in the procedure in the use of the Ulano "Hi-Fi" are: (1) exposing, (2) developing, (3) washing out, (4) adhering.

There is no special step in sensitizing, this being the distinguishing feature of presensitized films (Figure 51).

Exposing

The emulsion side of the positive is placed in contact with the plastic base of the film so that the light passes through the positive first.

A 35 amp. arc at a distance of 36 inches should produce a good film with a three-minute exposure. A 15 or 20 amp. arc at 20 inches should take about 6 minutes. These are only guiding estimates. Actual timing here, as in all photo film methods, depends upon variable factors. A test should precede an important job. That is a policy followed even by the most experienced operators.

Developing

The Ulano presensitized film uses one developing solution made from two packaged powders, called A and B. The solution is prepared by mixing one ounce (28 grams) of A to one ounce of B in one pint of water. Shake this in a covered bottle until both powders are in complete solution. (Temperature of water is not important— it may be cold, or warm, but never over 80°F.). Pour this developer into a tray. Mix just about enough for one day's use. The mixture does not have any holding power.

Place the exposed film (film side up) in the developer. Soon the developing bath changes color, showing that chemical action is taking place. Activate this process by rocking the tray so that the solution flows freely over the film. The film is ready for the next step, which is the wash out.

Washing Out

Place the film in a tray of warm water about 100° to 115° F. Continue this until the film image is clearly visible. Rinse with cold water (tray or gentle spray) and fasten to the screen in the usual manner described before. The procedure for filling in and stripping the backing sheet is the same as before described.

Conversion of Presensitized Screens

A chemical action induced by heat or a special solvent is necessary to fortify this type of photo stencil for unusually long runs, as for industrial printing of containers, printed circuits, etc. There are two ways to accomplish this "conversion."

1. *The heat method.* This employs the use of an electric iron, set to the "Wool" temperature control. Place the screen on a smooth and hard surface such as plate glass, masonite, metal plate, etc. and iron the inside of the screen for several minutes. Repeat this action on the film side by building up the "pack up" so that the silk rests firmly on a base. When the film changes to a purplish cast the action has been completed.

2. *The solvent method.* This is for silk and fabric screens only, not for nylon, dacron or other synthetic fabrics. A special solvent sold by the dealer is available for this purpose. Since this solvent has toxic properties, care must be taken not to get it on the bare hands. The prescribed method is to dip a piece of absorbent cotton in the solution, using a pair of tongs, and apply the solution to the inside of the screen, completely covering the film area, then repeat this on the film side. After five minutes, wipe the screen on the inside using a dry pad of cotton or soft cloth. Allow to dry and set overnight.

Conversion of the screen is a precaution against breakdown of this type of photo film and is intended for industrial printing of very large runs and continuous day-in and day-out use. The procedure is somewhat involved, but the time spent assures the longevity of the stencil, a condition very important in industrial printing.

One of the drawbacks of this type of conversion-fixed stencil is that the film cannot be removed from the stencil fabric. It is that durable. Once the stencil is made, the design cannot be dissolved from the mesh.

The Ulano "Hi-Fi" film described above can be stored away almost indefinitely without breaking down or becoming brittle. Should unusual weather conditions cause an indication of brittleness, the following solution, applied to the screen, will stop any such breakdown: 85 parts of isopropyl alcohol, 10 parts of water, and 5 parts of glycerine. The problem of making the screen so durable is of particular concern to specialized industrial users rather than to the average poster printer.

THE DUPONT PRESENSITIZED FILM

This film incorporates some of the features of the Ulano "Hi-Fi" film just discussed. The DuPont film however, has a unique additional feature: no transparency or positive is needed. The film is so fast that the image can be projected from the art work itself directly to the film, thus obviating the need of the positive.

Important steps are listed below.

Exposing

Since the speed of the emulsion is high, exposure may be made by contact or projection and is always made *through* the vinyl backing sheet of the film. Because of its fast speed and high sensitivity to light, a darkroom is essential. In the darkroom, the film is handled under red safe-lights such as Wrattan No. 1A. There are three methods of exposure: The exposure can be made with a copy camera using a yellow Wrattan No. 4 filter. The second method is by optical projection, using a good enlarger with a fine lens. The third method is by the customary contact printing. Exposure time will depend upon the nature of the light, distance from copy, etc. Tests will build up experience and judgment here.

Developing

After the film is exposed it may be immediately developed, or this may be deferred. Of course, covered storage space must be provided which shelters the exposed film from light or dust. A two-part developer of packaged chemicals is provided for this purpose, made especially for this film.

Steps in developing are: First, immerse the film in a tray of developing solution "A" for one minute, to absorb the developing agent. No developing action takes place here. Then, transfer the film to activator "B" for one minute. You will see the photographic image appear quickly. Next, rinse the developed film in tap water for about 20 seconds to remove excess developer. Last, bathe the film for 20 seconds in a five per cent acid stop bath. This arrests further developing and the remaining light sensitivity is completely destroyed. White lights can then be turned on.

Washing Out

The wash out step is accomplished quickly by directing a stream of hot water onto the film until the unexposed, unhardened emulsion is removed completely. A shower spray, gently directed, is recommended.

Adhering

The adhering of the photo film to the screen is accomplished in the usual manner, by placing the film (gelatin side up) under the screen, lowering the screen to establish good contact between film and silk, and applying even pressure throughout. There is no danger here of too firm an application of pressure during the blotting, as pressure cannot squash the hardened gelatin layer. From this step on, filling in the screen, peeling the backing sheet, etc. are identical with the Ulano "Hi-Fi" method previously described.

THE KODAK EKTAGRAPH FILM

There are various other photo stencil presensitized films among which the Ektagraph film, a Kodak product, is widely used. Space limitations do not permit me to describe here the various steps in detail, nor would it serve any purpose, because detailed instructions can be had in printed form by writing to the Eastman Kodak Company, Rochester, New York. Suffice it to say that there are four major steps consisting of (1) exposure, (2) developing, (3) washing out, (4) adhering. The entire procedure takes considerably less than half an hour, from positive to the ready-to-print stencil. Excellent results attest to the success of this Kodak product as a standard method in screen process photography.

There is practically no technical limitation to the inherent potential of the photographic stencil process for reproducing the finest line drawings and minuscule type matter. Discussion and conflict may arise, however, when the photo screen process is considered for fine halftone and four-color process. The boasts that silk screen can duplicate the effect of halftone and color lithography cannot as yet be substantiated. Although for many years four-color halftone has been printed by screen process, the practice has for the most part been limited geographically to one area of the United States, principally the Middle West. Even there, the results do not put lithography to shame. Some excellent examples of four-color screen process printing may be seen exhibited at conventions and trade shows, but these display pieces are not yet typical of nationwide trade standards. However, it can be said without fear of refutation that when it comes to line reproduction, the photographic process has developed high standards of craftsmanship comparable to the highest standards of the more traditional printing processes, and with a quality uniquely its own.

TEN THINGS TO REMEMBER IN PHOTO SCREEN WORK

1. Read carefully the instructive literature which you get with the purchase of packaged photo stencil material. The step-by-step procedure may vary with each supplier because of different chemical formulations.

2. For getting perfect results, a vacuum frame is a great help. However, for a beginner doing an occasional photo screen, a well-padded, heavy duty contact frame is satisfactory.

3. Check the candlepower of your exposure light. A carbon arc lamp is best and most stable. Fotoflood bulbs may be used; however, they gradually lose their intensity and may throw your exposure table off schedule.

4. Be sure your screen fabric is scrupulously clean and free from grease, dust and oily residues. Make it a matter of routine

to give the screen a thorough hot water scrubbing with Ajax, Oakite, or a similar cleansing product.

5. Do not guess at the timing. Get a good timer. The General Electric X-Ray Corporation of Milwaukee makes a good one.

6. Make test shots before proceeding with an important job. Chemicals and lights are not always stable. Humidity and other weather changes require a flexible exposure schedule.

7. Absolute cleanliness is essential. Dust or grime on film, or on positives, exposure glass and trays may explain the presence of pinholes, or difficulty in adhesion.

8. In using fast films, a darkroom or light-proof curtained work space is necessary. Use amber safety light for working illumination.

9. Read the supplier's instruction sheet for special care in handling chemicals to which you may be allergic. It is a good policy to make use of photographer's gloves and tongs, which can be purchased at photo supply stores.

10. Use measuring devices and thermometers to get the accuracy prescribed in the instructions. Do not guess or estimate when you should time, measure or weigh.

A WORD ABOUT POSITIVES

There may be a conflict in meaning when this term is used photographically. The technical parlance refers to a photographic transparency as a "negative"—a word which to some has become synonymous with all photographic transparencies. We, in the silk screen process field, require a *positive*. That is where the black parts on the black-and-white art appear as *black* opaque areas on the transparency. This entails two stages in photographing art work. The first stage is a negative; the second stage is a positive.

There are two principal ways of producing positives: (1) photographic and (2) hand-prepared methods.

(1) *Photographic positives*. This is a camera-prepared image, generally on an acetate, vinyl, or other plastic transparency. A well prepared photo positive will be as sharp as the original art and can be made same size, larger or smaller than the art work.

More and more of the larger screen shops now produce their own camera-made positives. Others use the available services of photoengraving establishments.

(2) *Hand-made positives.* There are two ways of preparing hand-made positives. One is to brush in the image on a sheet of acetate or other transparency, using a dense india ink or photo-engraver's opaquing ink. The techniques range from free-flowing strokes made by brush or litho crayon to stipple, spatter, dry brush, and other art treatments. It must be borne in mind that the painted-in areas must be *opaque*, and not merely washes or stains.

In addition to using ink, paint, or crayon with brush or pen, excellent positives may be prepared by using a special ruby-colored hand-cut film which is manufactured for that purpose. This film, sold under the trade name Fotomask, cuts and strips exactly as standard hand-cut film tissues. The main difference is in the color of the film. Since ruby or any reddish color photographs black, a stencil cut with red film makes an excellent positive for photo screen work. Still another way, somewhat similar to the hand-cut film described above, is the Bourges film (described in Chapter 19). This, like the hand-cut film, is transparent and available in red. The only difference here is that the Bourges film surface is not cut and stripped with a stencil knife. Instead, it is scraped away with a stylus or washed away with a special solvent. It is advisable to experiment with both and use each where most expedient.

5. MULTICOLOR WORK

SO FAR we have been concerned with the *techniques* of various stencil making methods without regard to color separations, or multicolor work. But since screen process is basically a separate stencil-per-color process, multicolor art work, to be reproduced faithfully, in most cases requires an individual stencil to correspond to each color shown on the art work. There are exceptions to this, as we shall see later, but for the time being, let us assume that we want to print a simple two-color design which will require two stencils. How to prepare each of these two stencils and get them to register in the print will be our present task. To make the instruction simple and perhaps all the more meaningful, let us assume that the art work consist of an 11" x 14" card on which a yellow rectangle appears bounded by a 1" black border all around it.

Also, let us agree that we will use the hand-cut film method, and that we will print with opaque poster paints. This will simplify matters both in describing the procedure and in understanding it.

PREPARATION FOR TWO-COLOR DESIGN

1. *Draw register marks on the art.* Within the margins on the card surrounding the design, carefully draw in four hairline cross marks, like the fine crosses on a gun sight. These may be done in pencil or ink and will serve as register marks for both making the stencils and printing the job.

2. *Choose a sequence of colors.* There is no hard and fast rule

in the matter of which color to print first. Here, however, are two guide posts:

(a) In printing with opaque paints, the background or the larger areas of the art are generally printed first. In the hypothetical job we have chosen, we would make the yellow background color No. 1, and the black frame color No. 2.

(b) The lighter colors are generally printed before the darker. This, however, though true in printing with transparent paints, does not necessarily follow when printing with opaque paint. Theoretically, in screen process, a light opaque paint can adequately cover over a dark background. For instance, you can print white lines over a black background with good coverage.

3. *Keep sequence notation.* Once you have chosen the color sequence, neatly list it within the outside margin of the design. Thus, our hypothetical job will show the following: Color Sequence—#1 Yellow, #2 Black. This sequence notation becomes very important when the jobs are in many colors, as the printing of each must follow the same order as the corresponding stencil sequence.

4. *Cut the first color.* Cut a piece of film large enough to include the register crosses and tape it (lacquer side up) securely over the art. Cut the yellow rectangle, making the boundaries go about ⅛" into the black frame. This "overdraw," which makes the yellow rectangle larger, assures that it will be more than big enough to extend into the black when printed. The black frame (the color to follow), being printed in an opaque color, will cover the "overdraw" and assure that no white will peep through where black and yellow are to meet.

Now cut the four crosses, making the lines no heavier than they appear on the art.

5. *Strip the film* within the cut areas. Don't forget to strip the crosses as well. For all practical purposes, the crosses are part of the design.

6. *Mark the color and number on the film.* Using a ball point pen which will take on the smooth surface of the film, write down the sequence of the color. In this case, it will say: #1 yellow.

This is necessary so that the stencils may be readily identified when several or more are pre-cut long before they are made to adhere.

7. *Put stencil under screen.* Place the art, film still attached to it, within the register guides set on the printing base.

8. *Lower the screen;* adhere the film in this fixed position.

9. *After the backing sheet is stripped* and the surrounding silk is properly filled in, the stencil is ready for squeegee and paint.

When the art work is released, back to your stencil cutting table it goes, where you proceed to cut color No. 2, black. The cutting procedure for this is identical, with one exception. You do not over-draw. The black is made exact, since no color is to follow it. Again you cut design and crosses, strip the film, identifying color and sequence, adhere the stencil, etc. This would be the identical procedure to follow if this job were not merely in two, but in many colors. The step-by-step method is the same, though of course many judgments would enter in for complicated color separation of multi-color work.

MAKING MULTICOLOR STENCILS
FOR TRANSPARENT COLOR PRINTING

For printing with transparent colors, the sequence must be arranged so that the light colors are printed first. To illustrate with an simple example: Let us say that the art to be reproduced shows yellow lettering over a black background. It would be no trouble at all, of course, to use opaque paints, print a black background first and then print opaque yellow over it. That we know. But let us say that there is some special reason why you want to use transparent colors, as for instance a transparent fluorescent yellow on a black ground. In this case, the first stencil to be cut (and first color to be printed) would be yellow. In making the yellow stencil, the lettering would have to be cut slightly fatter or overdrawn about 1/16″ all around. The stencil for the next color, black, would be made exact, overlapping into the yellow and reducing the lettering to the original size. This overdraw serves as a margin of safety or "catch-all" to assure alignment between one color and another.

"Trapping" Colors with the Use of Transparencies

There are occasions, however, when we do *not* want one color to hide another, when in fact, we want transparent effects. Some beautiful effects can be achieved by intentionally arranging the sequence so that a transparent color is made to overlap another color with a resultant multiple tone or completely new color in the overlapped area. To simplify with an example: Suppose a solid transparent yellow circle is made to overlap half into another circle of blue. The overlapping area would be green. A red area printed over a yellow would produce a shade of orange. A red over black would turn into brown, turquoise blue over a cerise would produce a purple, and so on. You get the same effect in overprinting with transparent colors as you would in overlapping transparent colored films over one another.

With the proper sequence, it is possible to get as many as eight different colors and tones with as few as four stencils and four printings. Many colorful multicolor posters are produced by using transparent colors with few actual printings. Why then is this method not more widely used? Why limit yourself to opaque colors which require a separate stencil and separate printing for each color? There are several reasons. First, when printing with transparent colors, we must always start with a white background. Transparent colors printed over a dark background would lose their brilliance or even their identity. One of the features of screen process is that we can print on *any* material, *any* surface and on *any* color. This holds true with opaque colors, not with transparencies. Another limitation to using transparent colors is that the results of overlapping are somewhat unpredictable. A certain shade of yellow over a certain shade of blue will produce a distinct kind of green, but that green may not match the exact shade of green on the art work, because the blue and the yellow on the art may not be the right tones to produce, in combination, the desired green. In opaque colors, on the other hand, a true match is possible. The color is matched to the art exactly as the artist did it when he painted the art work. Each opaque color is matched directly to the art with controllable fidelity. The color in the paint pot looks exactly as it does on the print.

SPLIT FOUNTAIN

Two colors may be printed at the same time from the same screen if the color areas are separated by about two inches or more. To accomplish this, the screen is partitioned off by means of a cardboard separator so that a different color may be poured into each compartment. A separate squeegee is used for each and thus the printing of both colors can be done simultaneously. In the parlance of the graphic arts, this is called "split fountain" printing. A split fountain arrangement may be used for any number of colors which are spaced widely enough to allow room for partitions between them.

GRADUAL BLEND EFFECT

The best reproducible art for screen process is that where each color is distinct and kept within a clearly defined boundary, in poster technique. It is possible, though, for some limited blending effects to be achieved, though the attainment of such an effect is difficult and time-consuming. It is possible, for instance, to get a gradual airbrush blend from one tone to another, but the gradation must be parallel to the direction of the squeegee movement. For instance, to simulate a blended sky, from deep blue on top to pale blue at the horizon, several different blues would be required, ranging from deep blue to a medium blue and a pale blue. These would be carefully placed into the screen in successive order, and squeegeed evenly across the screen. The first few prints would show distinct bands of different blues, but as the printing operation continues, the colors within the screen would gradually run into each other and blend to produce a print corresponding to the mixed values of the colors within the screen. This blend would be unstable. It would change from print to print as the colors within the screen run into each other more and more. No two prints would be exactly alike. After 20 or 30 prints, the colors would be so intermixed in the screen that the blend would diminish until the color would finally end up as a common intermixture. To avoid that, the different blues in their proper sequence would have to be replaced to revive the original effect. You can see that this entails a rather tedious operation, not paced to the pressure of speed in commercial production. This blending is an experimental effect suitable for limited editions where speed and cost are not important factors.

MULTI-BLEND EFFECT

In the gradual blend technique described above, care would have to be exercised to direct the movement of the squeegee evenly to effect an evenly blended print. There are cases, however, where an effect is desired where shades of the same color, or non-analogous colors run into each other quite haphazardly in free flowing marble-like patterns. This effect can be achieved by merely placing various colors into the screen and squeegeeing them through the stencil without regard to subtlety or refinements of blend. Naturally, it would be extremely difficult to exercise any control over the constantly changing intermixture of the paint within the screen. Whereas some prints may turn out to be surprisingly pleasing, the results cannot be kept constant. These "tricky" effects are commendable for experimental serigraphers and print makers but not much can be said for their practicality in commercial printing.

It may not be amiss at this time to ask you to turn to Chapter 18, "How to Prepare Art for Screen Process," to fix in your mind the importance of always suiting the art technique to the printing process and the advantages of staying within the bounds of practicality.

6. MAKE-READY, PRINTING, AND WASH UP

MAKE-READY

BEFORE THE actual printing is started, certain preparatory steps collectively called "make-ready" are necessary to assure the best production conditions and quality controls. This means the register guides must be properly set, the stencil checked, the squeegee properly selected, proofs pulled and approved, and so on. In general printing terminology, "make-ready" is more or less confined to "lock up" of type, tympan adjustment on the plate and register adjustment. In screen process, however, the term is used more broadly and encompasses all the preparatory steps between the time the stencil is set into the hinges to the time the actual printing production begins. Let us follow a job through from the time the stencil is ready, to the printing of the proofs. Below is a listing of things to check.

The printing base. The base must be absolutely smooth and free from warpage. Any valleys or peaks in the baseboard would interfere with proper contact and result in troublesome printing. When using a wood base, it is a good policy to cover it with a protective coating of shellac or lacquer to keep it impervious to moisture or solvents.

Register guides. In screen process, we use the three-guide system of registration of colors. The guides may be made of cardboard, heavy acetate, tape or metal, and are firmly set on the base in the position shown in Figure 52. The nature of the stock and length of the run will determine the choice of guide material. For a short run

80

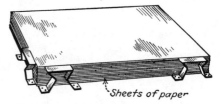

Sheets of paper

FIG. 52. Standard three-point guide system.

FIG. 53. Collapsible guides for stack feeding of paper.

of 50 to 100 cards, cardboard guides of a thickness not to exceed that of the printing stock should prove sufficient. On longer runs, the material selected for the guides must be more durable to withstand the constant wear and tear as the stock is fed against them. The slightest wearing away of the guides will prove disastrous, especially in multicolor work where extreme accuracy of register is of paramount importance. The guides, as we have said, must be no higher than the printing surface or else they will interfere with the proper contact. In general, metal slugs are used on long runs because they withstand best the constant pressure on the guides as the stock is butted against them. For running on light-weight paper, gum paper strips fastened to the base are all right. When printing paper, sometimes it is feasible to have a high feed of ten or more papers, well jogged and set into collapsible guides, as illustrated in Figure 53. This speeds up the feeding operation and is expedient where closeness of register is not crucial. For printing on unusually heavy stock, such as plate glass or wood panels, etc. the guides must be exceptionally strong. Also, the surrounding area on the base must be built up to avoid the bumping of the squeegee as it passes over the edges of the heavy material beneath.

The screen frame. Unless the frame is absolutely rigid, it may be subject to a twisting motion due to the pull of the squeegee during printing. Such a twist, no matter how imperceptible, would have a tendency to throw the stencil out of kilter and result in faulty registration of colors. Care must be exercised to check for frame rigidity *before* the stencil is applied. To try to correct that after the stencil has adhered may result in a twisted stencil image and consequent register distortion. Check against side-to-side sway of the screen frame. As an added precaution against any such development, there are two suggestions which will prove helpful. One is to drive a nail, dowel or pin through the frame, right into the bed. This will serve as an interlocking device. Another suggestion is to drive two small wood cleats on the base snug against each of the short sides of the frame. The frame in coming down will thus be wedged in, unable to be shifted once it is down on the base (see Figures 16 and 19). (Automatic screen presses are equipped with built-in controls against side-to-side twist.)

Hinges. Check the hinges to be sure that male and female units are firmly interlocked. If the component parts of the hinges are loose, or the pin that binds them is worn down, there will be a "play" in the hinged frame. Check to see that screws which hold the hinges are tight and grip the hinges tightly to the frame.

Squeegee. Select the squeegee with care. Squeegee rubber varies in flexibility, thickness and composition. The length of the squeegee should extend several inches beyond the width of the printing area. Be sure that the blade is as sharp as you want it; rubber dulls with constant use. A few passings over a sanding block will restore the edge. It is time-consuming to change squeegees after the job is started. It is wiser to exercise care in the selection *before* the run.

The stencil. The stencil should be thoroughly examined before it is considered ready for printing. The examination should include a careful check of the printing areas, possible presence of pinholes, blemishes in the stencil tissue or in the open silk, etc. It is faster and less messy to check the stencil *before* it is filled in with paint. It becomes an exasperating and time-costing experience to attempt to make corrections during the run with everybody nervously waiting around for the "repairs."

Color. Be it paint, lacquer, enamel or other media, color should not be put into the printing screen before it has been tested and approved for shade, printing viscosity, drying quality, texture, finish, etc. Tests should be made on a testing screen prior to handing over the entire batch of color to the printer. In a well organized screen shop pretesting of color is a routine procedure.

Proofing. The job is not ready for production until proofs are pulled, checked, and approved. Checking includes a final inspection of the accuracy of the stencil, accuracy of color match, and register. It may be necessary to make minor changes in relation to colors previously printed. Register guides may have to be shifted to align the color being printed with the preceding ones. Often "off register" may not be attributable to human carelessness at all. It may have been caused by infinitesimal changes in the stencil or the stock due to weather and humidity fluctuations. Whatever the cause, adjustments must be made to counteract these conditions and re-establish, correct and fix the register before proceeding with production.

PRINTING

The pushing of the squeegee across the screen is deceivingly simple. Any casual observer watching an experienced squeegee operator pushing a squeegee would be inclined to inquire, "Is that all there is to it?" Apparently, all one does is to insert a card, lower the frame and push the paint from one side of the screen to the other. It may seem incredible that such an apparently simple operational procedure should require extensive experience. But it does. While it is true that "anybody can push a squeegee," there is a right way to do it, and a wrong way. The right way will yield clear, sharp, well-registered prints; the wrong way will merely swish paint through the openings of the stencil resulting in blurry impressions lacking uniformity or sharpness of line, and with unreliable register.

A verbal description of the actual printing procedure necessarily falls short of an actual demonstration or personal instruction. But for the want of the latter, we shall attempt it.

The card (or other printing surface) is placed firmly in the guides set up on the base. The screen is lowered. Paint is poured into the right end of the screen. Now, firmly grasping the squeegee handle with the right hand, evenly and with uniform pressure, scrape the paint across the screen going from right to left. That completes one print. Now lift the screen, remove the card from the guides, and hand the wet print over to your assistant or "take off man." He will place the wet print on a conveyer belt leading to a drying oven or (in the absence of such heating equipment) into a drying rack. Insert another card, and lower the screen. Now grasp the squeegee with the left hand and scrape the paint evenly across the screen, going from left to right. Again, raise the screen, and lift the card off the base. Thus the cycle continues. Each squeegee crossing results in a print. One paint filling of the screen may last for 25 to 50 prints before it has to be replenished. Actually, only a given amount of paint is used up for each print regardless of the reservoir of paint in the screen. The amount of paint consumed for each print is determined by several factors: first, by the area of coverage which is determined by the stencil openings; then, by the condition of the squeegee rubber and the degree of pressure applied; the third and fourth factors are the absorbency of the printing surface and the mesh count of the screen fabric.

Care must be exercised in the feeding of stock into the printing guides. The slightest irregularity will throw that color out of kilter, a condition which will show up dramatically when the succeeding colors in a multicolor project are printed.

Care must also be shown throughout the run for the presence of any smears, blemishes, specks in the print, etc. These irregularities must be corrected immediately and not allowed to run on and on. Occasionally, the underside of the screen must be cleaned with a kerosene damp rag (if one uses oil base paints) to keep the underside free from any accumulation of lint from the material being printed.

A crew of two operating a manual unit can produce several hundred impressions per hour. The pace will of course vary with the size of the screen, the dimensions and nature of the printing surface, and the physical energy of the operators. Obviously, screening heavy plate glass requires more time and care than light-weight, easy-to-handle cardboard.

When the printing is done by a professional, it does not seem messy at all. In the hands of an amateur, silk screen seems a very messy procedure. The experienced squeegee pusher will seem to be unhurried, to work with a well regulated pace and to keep his hands, screen frame, and printing stock free from smudges. He is in perfect control of the situation. Isn't this the same with experienced practitioners of most other crafts?

WASH UP

When the printing is finished, a waste card or paper is placed on the printing base and the screen is ready for cleaning. The unused color remaining in the screen is scooped up with two pieces of stiff, sharp-edged cardboard handled in the manner of a V-shaped trough.

This leftover paint is put back in the original paint can, covered, properly identified and stored away. Now with a plentiful supply of soft absorbent waste rags handy, one large rag is saturated in kerosene and swooshed around in the screen, dissolving and absorbing the paint which clings to screen and open mesh. The screen is then lifted and another kerosene-soaked rag is similarly applied to the underside of the screen. This is followed up by a vigorous application of dry rags to the top and bottom of the screen, until all traces of paint or kerosene are completely removed from the entire screen —top, bottom, frame and all. The screen must be left absolutely spotless so that one could hardly discern what color had been printed with last. This scrupulous cleanliness is important, if the screen is to be reused at any future time.

Similar care in cleaning the squeegee must be exercised. Using a kerosene-soaked rag as a first application, all traces of paint must be dissolved and removed. This is followed by a dry-rag wipe to absorb any solvent. If paint is allowed to remain on the squeegee rubber, it becomes difficult to wash later. Furthermore, the hardened paint may crack the rubber blade, thus making the squeegee quite useless for further work. The entire operation of washing up the average size screen and squeegee need take no more than ten minutes, from start to finish.

Cleaning Solvents for Printing Compounds

We have mentioned kerosene in our instructions on cleaning the screen because that is a standard inexpensive solvent for most oil base paints used in screen process printing. As you will learn when you read the chapter on printing compounds, there is a variety of different printing compounds, such as enamels, lacquers and synthetics, all of which require compatible solvents for washing screens.

Here are some major printing compounds and their respective wash-up solvents:

Most oil base poster paints ....Mineral spirits, kerosene, varnolene, turps, naphtha.

Enamel paints ....Same as above.

Fluorescent paints ....Same as above.

Vinyl and other lacquer compounds ....Lacquer wash thinners.

Tempera (water base) paints ....Water.

DISSOLVING THE STENCIL

After the screen is cleaned, it may be stored away for re-use on a repeat job, or the stencil image may be dissolved, thus reclaiming the silk. This applies to the tusche stencil, the glue or shellac block-out stencil, the hand-cut lacquer film stencil and the hand-cut Pro-film shellac stencil. It applies only theoretically to the photo stencil and not at all to the paper stencil. A paper stencil cannot be saved and stored away for a future rerun. It is strictly a one-shot deal, but after the paper is removed, the silk screen is easily washed, and remains unimpaired.

How to Dissolve the Tusche-glue Stencil

The tusche-glue stencil must be thoroughly washed with cold or warm water, water being the solvent for glue. After all traces of glue have been dissolved, the screen is given another washing of water, after which it is dried with absorbent rags. The appearance of any cloudiness in the mesh is indicative of the presence of residual glue and therefore shows the need of a rewash and subsequent drying. A faint impression of the stencil image may appear on the screen. This, if it appears clear and open on the silk may merely be a dried residual stain caused by the paint and in no way interferes with the usefulness of the screen.

Tusche-glue resist stencils may be used with oil base poster paint, enamels, lacquers, and any other medium which does not contain water, or is water-soluble.

Dissolving Other Types of Stencils

The procedure here is the same as for the tusche-glue stencil; only the solvent differs. The solvent for lacquer stencils is wash lacquer thinner. The solvent for shellac stencils is alcohol. Although hot water and an enzyme preparation are the prescribed solvents for the removal of photo stencil film, it takes a lot of scrubbing to effect good results. Most practitioners in the field feel that the reclaiming of the silk is not worth the effort involved. The easiest screens to clean are the stencils made with hand-cut lacquer films and the glue methods. The job, done properly, is accomplished within a matter of minutes, leaving the silk clean and receptive for the new design or the next color in the sequence.

After the printing is done, the stencil image may be dissolved, or the screen, with stencil intact, may be stored away indefinitely for a future rerun. A stall is generally provided for the storage of stencils, each of which is properly labeled for easy reference.

7. FACTS ON SCREEN FABRICS

SILK WAS originally the only fabric employed for the silk screen process. Though silk is thus traditionally identified with this process, it is no longer the exclusive screen fabric used today. Among others are organdy, nylon, dacron, stainless steel, copper mesh, etc. As new uses are found for the screen process and new technical demands made by diversified inks and printing surfaces, various other fabrics are found to have some inherent advantages over the conventional silk. However, since silk is still the major fabric in the industry, we shall discuss that first.

SILK

All screen fabrics viewed under a magnifying glass can be seen as finely woven mesh strands, producing a porous surface (Figure 54). The finer the weave, the smaller the openings between the strands. This mesh count is identified by number, thus No. 6 would be coarse, No. 12 medium, No. 18 very fine, and so on. In silk, the number range varies from No. 6 to No. 25.

The best grade of silk is a fine bolting cloth material imported from Switzerland. It is made with a taffeta weave (interlocking basket weave construction) and has great tensile strength, is very durable and of great uniformity. It is also quite costly, with prices ranging from $6.00 to $10.00 per yard.

There are also a number of Japanese imports and domestic silks (sold under various trade names) which are less expensive and for most practical purposes serve just as well. These, too, have taffeta

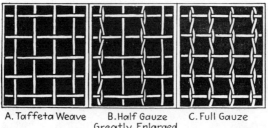

A. Taffeta Weave   B. Half Gauze   C. Full Gauze
Greatly Enlarged

FIG. 54. Magnified view of silk fabric weaves.

weaves and the necessary tensile strength to make them durable for many thousands of impressions.

Silk is identified by number and X or XX. The symbol XX means double extra and indicates the weight of the fabric. The number indicates the mesh count per linear inch, or the number of mesh openings per linear inch.

Mesh counts are as follows:

6xx = 73 meshes per linear in.	15xx = 144 meshes per linear in.
7xx = 81 " " " "	16xx = 152 " " " "
8xx = 85 " " " "	17xx = 160 " " " "
9xx = 95 " " " "	18xx = 170 " " " "
10xx = 106 " " " "	19xx = 175 " " " "
11xx = 114 " " " "	20xx = 180 " " " "
12xx = 122 " " " "	21xx = 185 " " " "
13xx = 127 " " " "	22xx = 200 " " " "
14xx = 136 " " " "	

DACRON AND NYLON

These synthetic man-made fabrics have excellent tensile strength and are fine for making direct contact photo screens. They are not widely used for hand-cut or transfer photo stencils because the strands are rather finely polished and so do not offer the natural anchorage that natural silk possesses.

ORGANDY

This is an inexpensive substitute for silk. Its main advantage is its comparatively low price. Organdy costs about $1.25 to $3.50 per yard, depending upon quality and width of yardage. It comes in widths of 40, 42, 53 and 60 inches and with only one standard mesh count of 109, equivalent to about No. 11 silk. Drawbacks in the use of organdy are the following: it does not have the resilience or tensile strength of silk, it is not as uniform in weave and it does not come in a complete range of mesh counts. Another serious limitation of organdy is that it tends to sag and lose its tautness on the frame, especially when exposed to water or humid weather conditions. This would not make it the recommended fabric for any printed medium which is water-soluble.

WIRE CLOTH

On some highly specialized industrial printing of indeterminable runs, it is advantageous to use wire cloth. This comes in a variety of types including bronze, copper, and stainless steel. Wire cloth is extremely durable, can be woven exceedingly fine and with controlled uniformity. It withstands the action of abrasive or caustic inks. It is easy to see why it is widely used for industrial screen printing of glassware, printed circuits, containers, etc. Stainless steel comes in 40″ widths and in meshes so fine that the fabric hardly looks porous at all, even if examined closely. Many of the very fine screen prints you may have admired on cosmetic containers, in lettering as small as 6 point type, most likely have been printed with stainless steel screen fabrics. Considering the durability of this material, the cost of such fabrics is not too high, the price ranging from $4.00 to $10.00 per yard, depending upon quantity purchased and the grade of mesh. Since such screens last almost indefinitely and are not above the cost of a good grade of imported silk, you may wonder why metal fabrics have not completely replaced silk for all screen process work. The reasons is that there are several inherent drawbacks to such screen fabrics. First, metal fabric is not as easily stretched as the more resilient and flexible silk. Then, too, because of its smooth non-absorbent surface, hand-cut screens do not adhere as well on metal screens as they do on silk. Still another limitation to wire screens is that the stencil cannot be washed off or dissolved as easily. In conclusion, it should be remembered that each screen fabric offers certain limitations and advantages and the experienced operator must know when to choose one in preference to another, as the need arises.

CARE OF THE SCREEN FABRIC

Most screen fabrics, when new, have an invisible deposit of wax, sizing agent, or other residual deposit connected with the process of weaving or manufacture. This residual matter must be removed after the fabric is attached to the screen frame. This is most important when using silk fabric intended for transfer photographic stencil films. If this residual deposit is not completely removed from the mesh, two things may happen. Either the stencil will refuse to adhere or else adhesion will be imperfect and the resulting stencil will break down during the printing. For this reason, manufacturers of the various photo transfer films as well as hand-cut films strongly recommend the following screen cleaning procedure.

Before the screen is ready to receive the stencil, be sure that you wash-scrub the fabric. Use plenty of hot water and scrub the silk on both sides using two suede brushes simultaneously, one on each side of the silk. The hot water bath should be followed up with an application of pumice-type household detergent powder solution, such as Oakite or Ajax. Then, rinse with cold water to remove all traces of the cleansing solution. Allow the fabric to dry.

If the action of the scrubbing produces a slight "tooth" or nap to the fibres, so much the better, provided of course that it does not result in rips or tears due to indiscriminate or too forceful a scrubbing action. A fine nap actually helps the subsequent adhesion of the film because it provides the necessary anchorage or gripping surface for the stencil tissue.

The measures outlined above for preparing *new* fabric apply equally well to silk or other fabric which is to be reused. Be sure that the previous stencil tissue is completely dissolved and that the silk appears absolutely clear. After this proceed on the assumption that the fabric may have lodged in its fibres an invisible deposit of oil, grease, or other solvent left over from the removal of the paint or the previous stencil. Then, as a matter of routine, scrub-wash the fabric with cleanser and hot water, following the instructions recommended for preparing a newly stretched screen.

8. STRETCHING SILK

THE "SCREEN" is the fabric stretched on a frame. In this short but important chapter, we will describe various ways of stretching the silk to produce the best printing screens. All other factors being equal, it is safe to say that the most tightly stretched screen yields the best printing results.

There is no one set way for stretching the silk (or other screen fabrics). Each technician likes to believe that the procedure he has developed is the "best," but the ways of doing the job vary. Until you develop your "best" individual techniques, follow this procedure.

STRETCHING THE SCREEN

The silk has no wrong or right side. Both sides are the same.

1. Set the screen frame on a sturdy table. Cut the silk several inches larger than the frame and place it over the frame. For fastening the fabric to the frame, you may use either tacks or staples. If you use tacks, get the standard No. 4 (about ¼" long) blue-black carpet tacks obtainable at any hardware or five-and-ten-cent store. If you prefer staples, use the heavy duty variety, the kind requiring a display tacker with a forceful hammer action. The procedure is the same whether you use tacks or staples (Figure 55).

2. Start at one of the long sides of the frame. Place a few tacks (or staples) at one end. Now pull the silk as hard as you can towards the other end and drive a few tacks into that end to keep the entire side taut. Be sure that the tacks are driven all the way down

FIG. 55. Heavy duty staple tacker for fastening the fabric to the frame.

into the frame. Remember that it is the top or head of the tack that anchors the silk and not the shank.

3. Drive in a row of tacks spaced about ½" apart, as shown in Figure 56, filling in the area between the two terminal sides bearing the tacks.

4. Now you are ready to stretch the opposite side. Starting at the center and pulling the silk as tightly as you can toward you, fasten it down in the taut position with several tacks. To stretch the rest of the side, pull the silk hard toward you and slightly toward one end. Fasten the silk down, one tack at a time, alternately from either side of the center. The pull is two-directional, toward you and toward one end of the frame. Continue in this fashion until the entire side is tightly stretched and tacked (Figure 57).

5. When the second long side is completely done, start at either one of the short sides. The procedure is the same. Again you start at the center and go towards the sides, alternately, until the entire side is finished (Figure 58).

6. The last side (Figure 59) is stretched the same way, again starting from the center and alternately going sideways. If the job is done right, the last stretch should remove any vestige of wrinkles or looseness in the fabric. A well stretched screen is as tight as a drum top—with practically no "give" or slackness whatever. The excess silk is then trimmed flush to the outer edges of the frame.

Side one.   Side two.

Side three.   Side four.

FIGS. 56–59. Stages in stretching the stencil fabrics.

The great pull of the silk sometimes has a tendency to force the fabric away from the tacks and cause it to rip at the mooring of the shank of the tack. To avoid this, some operators do not tack directly into the silk; instead they place a narrow (½″) cloth tape or band over the "hem" of the fabric and tack through this, the tape serving as a reinforcement track for the row of tacks.

BINDING THE SCREEN

After tacking, lacquer is brushed over the edges where silk meets wood. When the lacquer dries, it acts as an additional bond between the silk and wood frame. When this is completed, 2″ gum paper strips are glued down covering the entire surface of the tacked areas. The screen is turned over, and gum paper strips are folded in half and applied so that one half sticks to the inside of the frame, the other to the open silk. This gum paper binding, inside and out, prevents the possibility of paint oozing through between the silk and wood. The gum paper strips are brush coated with lacquer

FIG. 60. Special grip pliers for stretching screen fabrics. (*Courtesy Colonial Process Supply Co.*)

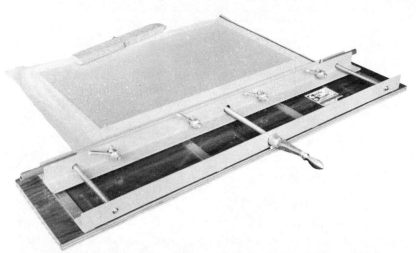

FIG. 61. The "Sparky" silk stretcher, a mechanical device for stretching silk. (*Courtesy Advance Process Supply Co.*)

to make them impregnable against paint or other printing media during the course of printing.

The procedure described above, though by no means the only way of doing the job, is adequate for the standard simple wood frames most commonly used in manually operated screen units.

There are several mechanical devices on the market designed to make the job of stretching screens less exerting and more efficient. Figure 60 shows a pair of special pliers for gripping the silk.

The mechanical silk stretcher shown in Figure 61 is a long metal bar with a rubber-edged double lip which grips the silk all along one end. By turning a crank, the metal bar moves toward you pulling the entire side of silk evenly, and resulting in a uniform

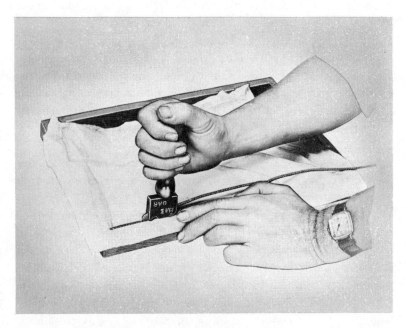

FIG. 62. Grooved frame and mechanical wedger which sets the silk and cord within the grooves of the frame. (*Courtesy Naz-Dar Co.*)

stretch. These mechanical stretching devices are sold under trade names, such as Sparky, Ward, etc.

Another mechanical silk-stretching device consists of an all-metal chase or frame with four floating bars within the frame. By turning a crank or butterfly nut, the four loose inner bars are drawn toward the outer chase; thus the inner "frame" in effect becomes larger. This inner frame has a gripping lip which holds the silk as the frame "expands." The silk gripped in this mechanically tight manner is then, by transfer, fastened over a frame. When completely attached, the frame is removed from the chase.

Another way of stretching screens makes use of a special grooved frame (Figure 62). This method does not require tacks or staples of any kind. Instead, it employs a tight-fitting cord which is wedged firmly into the grooves within the frame. The cord holds the fabric locked within the grooves. This type of frame has an added advantage; the silk may be removed from the frame by merely lifting out the cord, leaving the frame free for a new screen.

Still another method works on a completely different and rather novel principle. This does not use a conventional frame at all. Originally developed in Germany, this method works on the pneumatic principle of air pressure. Pneumatic frames are widely used for hard-to-stretch screen fabrics such as copper and stainless steel cloth. They theoretically produce the ultimate in screen tautness.

It is perhaps best to think of the pneumatic frame as a "square" bicycle tire. When loose, it is flexible. When inflated, it expands and becomes rigid.

The pneumatic frame is made from hardened aluminum alloy tubing equipped with strong corner pieces. Around it, serving as an outer tube, is the pneumatic "tire." The silk is gripped by a special device to the inner frame. This screen tire is inflated with air with the use of a common bicycle pump or similar device. As the tire expands, it grips the silk toward it, thus stretching the silk. By utilizing air pressure which equalizes automatically, it is possible to stretch screen fabrics quickly and without physical effort. The compressed air, pumped into the tire, stretches the screen to a tympan-like hardness unequalled by any other method. To release the fabric, the air is merely "let out." The release of air makes the pneumatic tire frame contract; the grippers are then opened and the fabric is then freed from the frame. The fabric bearing the stencil image may thus be filed flat or rolled up for re-use. It may be re-attached to the frame when needed.

Frame sizes (inside dimensions) vary from 16¾" by 22¼" to 24" by 27¾". Other sizes available go up to 50" by 70". Pneumatic frames used in conjunction with stainless steel fabric provide the ultimate in screens required for the finest and most durable stencil printing in the industry.

By comparison with the cost of standard wood frames, pneumatic tire frames are expensive and require a specialized setup for hinging and printing. This is one of the reasons why pneumatic screens are reserved mostly for mass volume industrial printing of mass production circuit electronics, ceramic or industrial container ware, etc. For all practical routine purposes, the simple wood frames described previously are still the standard of that large segment of the screen process industry devoted to advertising and display printing.

In all methods of screen stretching, the screen is not yet considered ready for use when the fabric has been tacked onto the frame. The fabric must in addition be scrub-washed to make it ready to receive the stencil. See Chapter 7 for procedure for washing the screen. This wash, in the case of silk and nylon, accomplishes another purpose. The water has a shrinking effect on the material and makes the fabric contract. In its contraction, the screen becomes all the more taut.

9. FACTS ABOUT PAINTS, LACQUERS AND OTHER PRINTING COMPOUNDS

THE POROUS surface of the silk screen will allow any viscous or gelatinous compound to go through the meshes when forced through with the pressure of a squeegee. The thinner the compound, the faster it will penetrate. The printing media used in commercial screen printing are of a paste or jelly consistency. These include paints, enamels, lacquers, dye, etc. However, the process is not limited to these alone. Varnish, glue, etching compounds, adhesives for tinsel, flock and other appliqués—all are compatible with the process and have wide industrial applications quite remote from conventional uses of the advertiser. We will deal with most of these in this chapter.

Fortunately, the silk screen printer today does not have to be an experimental amateur paint chemist to prepare his colors. Not that a knowledge of fundamental paint chemistry would be superfluous, but the fact of the matter is that it is not vital. This was not always so. Years ago, before screen process had grown into a major industry, each processor had to formulate his own paints, and often laboriously grind his own pigments, simply because there were no ready-to-use paints manufactured which were professionally formulated to his varied needs. Today, there are ready-to-use paints available for practically every screening purpose. There are colors specifically made for vinyl and other plastic surfaces. You may order by catalog number paints for printing on paper, cardboard, glass, metal. There are ceramic colors for baking and firing, colors

FIG. 63. A sampling of the multitude of containers which are effectively screened with specially prepared paints formulated for the purpose. (*Courtesy Wornow Process Paint Co., Los Angeles.*)

that are formulated to be opaque and others to dry with a clear transparency. You can get paints that will dry with a dull pastel finish; equally available are those which dry with a high gloss. The job of the color man in the contemporary screen shop has changed from that of amateur paint chemist to paint matcher and mixer. His work in the main consists of matching and testing colors, intermixing them with prescribed thinners and reducers, and selecting the proper type of colors for the specific job.

Before we proceed, I would like to call attention to the fact that I have used the terms paints, colors and inks interchangeably. Though that is the accepted practice in the loose trade terminology, I shall henceforth make free use of the generic term *color* with the understanding that it will have collective reference to paints, inks, dyes, lacquers, etc. as the case may be.

Without getting too involved in technical jargon, let us briefly review the structural composition of all process color. This consists in the main, of two major parts, the *vehicle portion,* a combination of various resins, oils and solvents. This is the fluid portion of the ink and acts both as a carrier and binder for the other part, which is the *pigment.* This latter part consists of the actual color particles as well as inerts. Inerts are colorless, transparent powders

FIG. 64. Example of plastic molded sign silk screened with special paints to withstand the heat and pressure of the forming process. (*Courtesy Chicago Show Printing Co., Chicago.*)

FIG. 65. The versatility of silk screen printing is exemplified in these bowling pins, machine printed with a special abrasion-proof paint and photo stencils. (*Courtesy Eastman Kodak Co.*)

that are added for bulk as well as to improve working qualities. The resin and oil portion together with the pigments comprise the solids, which may run as high as 80 per cent of the mixed color. The other 20 per cent consists of the volatiles. The solids are that portion of the color which remains behind as a dried film after the volatiles have evaporated.

CLASSIFICATION OF COLORS

All colors (this includes lacquers, inks, paints, enamels, etc.) can be classified into two major categories, depending upon the manner in which drying takes place. These categories are: (1) non-oxidizing types (2) oxidizing types.

Non-Oxidizing Color

This includes lacquer, ethyl cellulose inks, vinyl paints and a number of the poster paints and synthetics so popular today. All of these have one thing in common: they all dry by evaporation of

FIG. 66. A very colorful promotion folder screened with semi-gloss paints on a smooth coated stock. A combination of good design and good printing. (*Courtesy McCann Erickson, New York.*)

the solvents. No chemical process is involved. It is simply that the volatile elements having done their job as a carrier for the pigments, dry off, leaving a film of color on the surface. The paint chemist can hasten or retard the drying by the choice and quantity of the compatible solvents he intermixes with the pigment. He cannot use too fast a solvent, for obviously anything that dries rapidly on paper is going to dry just as rapidly, if not more so, in the meshes of the screen fabric. In a fast automatically operated press this is not too important a factor because the printing is done at such a fast pace that the paint is kept in constant agitation and does not remain idle on the screen.

Of course, the science of paint technology is not so simple as all that. The chemist has at his disposal hundreds of different resins, oils, inerts and solvents. The selection and proportions are crucial to the results.

A print made with non-oxidizing color can be force-dried by

FIG. 67. An excellent example of a single color halftone screen job printed from a Kodak Ektagraph photo stencil. (*Courtesy Eastman Kodak Co.*)

circulating air, heat or a combination of both, since drying takes place by evaporation.

Oxidizing Color

This type of color dries by a chemical action called oxidation. This is a phenomen similar to the oxidation of metals when exposed to air, resulting in rust. There the oxygen in the air combines with the metal to form a new compound in the form of rust. An oxidizing ink or paint does not rust, but it does contain lead, cobalt, zinc, manganese, or other metals, which, when they combine with oxygen, produce a chemical action whose outward manifestation is the drying or hardening of the ink film. Each of the varied metals used induces its own particular qualities in the drying action of paint. Cobalt, for instance, causes the paint film to dry from the bottom up. The chemical ramifications are too technical to be of practical value to the average paint mixer. The chemical balances of the component ingredients are so involved that the matter is better left to the professional chemists.

An oxidizing color contains volatiles and solvents which must evaporate just as for a non-oxidizing film but with this main difference: When all the volatiles have been evaporated from a non-oxidizing film, it is dry; but when they have evaporated from an oxidizing film, the drying action is just starting. This means that an oxidizing film must receive plenty of fresh circulating air or it will not dry. Heat is helpful because it promotes evaporation and accelerates the chemical process of oxidation, thus hastening the drying. The tendency in modern paint formulation is away from paints, inks, or lacquers which depend solely upon oxidation for drying.

POSTER COLORS

The scope of screen process is so large and its applications so varied that no one paint or ink could possibly satisfy all the requirements of the job on hand. Paint that is formulated for printing on cardboard is fine for cardboard, but may not be good for glass, cloth, vinyl, etc. Paint whose chemical formula is designed to work as an adhesive for flock is not meant to be used for printing on ceramics. Due to the great variety of printing media, which include paints, enamels, inks, lacquers, etc., it would be impractical to describe them all here. Our purpose at this point will be fulfilled if we review some of the main categories of colors or "lines" (as the dealers call them) and suggest that the interested reader make further researches on any special color by sending away for brochures from suppliers listed in Chapter 23.

Poster colors are divided into several subcategories, or "lines," which include (1) opaque colors, (2) transparent colors, (3) colors that dry with a pastel or matte finish, (4) colors that dry with a gloss, (5) colors which are formulated for normal air drying, (6) colors specially formulated for forced drying by oven or jet air.

Opaque Color Line

This line is variously referred to as poster paints or process paints. This color is a paste-like oil base paint which has the special property of opacity. With such paints you can print a light color over a dark background quite as easily as a dark color over a light one. Incidentally, this feature of opacity is among the most compelling selling points of the screen process industry. Hardly any other printing process can accomplish this as successfully. Lithography, letterpress, and other methods apply a thin film of transparent ink, while the screen process prints a layer of opaque paint.

Screen process opaque paints are available which under normal atmospheric conditions air-dry in racks in from 20 to 40 minutes. The colors dry by evaporation and may either be air-dried or oven-dried. Though most paints may be subjected to either air or oven drying, it is recommended here, as it is strongly urged by the manufacturers, that for best results the paint be selected specifically for one means of drying or the other. A paint intended for oven drying can be printed at the rate of more than 2000 impressions an hour and dried just as fast with the proper oven facilities.

The color range is extensive (some manufacturers list 50 different colors and tones) and all colors may be intermixed to produce an infinite color palette. Coverage is 800–1200 square feet per gallon. Each line has its own reducers and varnishes. Opaque colors can be had in either flat or velvet finish, semi-gloss or high mirror-like gloss. Poster colors are primarily intended for cardboard and paper.

FIG. 68. Colorful advertising over-the-wire banners screened with fast-drying oil base paints. (*Courtesy Interstate Boochever Corp., Fairlawn, N. J.*)

FIG. 69. A special paint is used to print on cork, such as the sample shown above.

Transparent Color Line

There are effects obtainable with transparent colors which duplicate in quality those obtained by color lithography. The most important advantage of using transparent colors is the multiple color effect achievable for surprinting (printing one color overlapping onto another). Whereas most silk screen opaque colors can be made transparent by the addition of a jelly-like substance called transparent base, the best results are achieved by using a line of transparent paints made for the purpose. These colors dry by evaporation and may be air or oven-dried. They air dry in approximately 15 to 20 minutes, oven dry in a matter of seconds. Transparent paints may be used straight from the can but a thinning agent is in the form of a varnish or reducer made for the purpose.

LUMINOUS COLORS

There are several major categories: (1) *Daylight fluorescent* colors, used in advertising. These have a high chromatic potency which makes them almost vibrate with intensity. (2) *Phosphorescent paints*, the kind used on radium-printed watch dials. These paints emit an after-glow of varying duration in the dark. Of these, there are two types: one is yellow-green in color and glows 15 to 20 minutes. This is primarily used on wall plaques, pictures and novelties. The other, medium blue in color, has a 12-hour afterglow and is used on exit signs, road markers, luminous watch dials, etc. (3) *Reflective paints* are used mostly on road signs. These "bounce off" light in a luminous glow activated by beams of automobile headlights. All of these can be grouped in a general category of luminous colors.

Daylight Fluorescence

Daylight fluorescent paints, sold under such trade names as Dayglo, Velva-Glo, Lumi-Glo, Day-lite, etc., take on a fluorescence under a black light but they are also activated by ordinary daylight, hence their name. These paints possess a natural visibility and chromatic power four times that of conventional paint. This visibility is

FIG. 70. A good photoscreen and finely ground screen paint formulated for fine halftone work helped to produce the excellent photographic screen print shown above. (*Courtesy Eastman Kodak Co.*)

actually strengthened on foggy or overcast days, when the glow emitted by these colors seems all the more vibrant.

Fluorescent colors possess the unique ability to absorb the sun's rays, as well as invisible ultra violet light energy, and to convert these into the form of visible color. In addition, fluorescents have a strong reflective chroma of their own. Since this new species of paint was first commercially developed about 1950, constant improvements have been made in quality, coverage, retaining power and extension of the color palette. A leading manufacturer's list consists of 8 colors: Aurora Pink, Neon Red, Rocket Red, Fire Orange, Blaze Orange, Arc Yellow, Saturn Yellow, and Signal Green.

When daylight fluorescent paint was in its early stages of development, it was characterized by a number of shortcomings, now almost completely overcome. Because the pigments used in fluorescent color are hard and glass-like in nature and require fine grinding in their formulation, the paints at first were somewhat rough-textured in both their liquid and printed state. As a consequence, a coarse No. 6 or No. 8 mesh screen was necessary to permit good penetration. Today, fluorescent paints are available which are as smooth as conventional colors. They work well with a No. 10 or No. 12 or even finer mesh, dry smoothly and quickly and yield a coverage of 800 to 1000 square feet of printing area per gallon. The "mileage" or coverage will naturally depend upon a number of factors. The coarser the screen mesh used, the more paint will be laid on any given area, and consequently, the less mileage can be expected. Other factors are the absorbent surface of the printing material. You will get less coverage on absorbent spongy board than you will on a hard, smooth-coated stock. The squeegee pressure, too, will influence the consumption of paint. These factors, it must be pointed out, apply not only to fluorescent paints, but to all standard colors as well.

It is well to remember that the thicker the layer of fluorescent paint, the brighter and longer-lasting the glow will be when exposed to sunlight. A three-month exposure life can be expected from daylight fluorescent paints with one coat of paint. Two coats will double the duration of this color. However, this time table is qualified by weather conditions and geographic locations. A fluorescent poster exposed in the blistering sun of the deep South will fade faster than the same poster displayed in the more temperate climate of Chicago or New York.

Just as there is a wide variety of standard paints for varied materials and uses, there are now fluorescent colors made for specific surfaces. For instance, for printing on vinyl film, pyroxylin-coated fabrics and other plastic materials, there is a fluorescent lacquer formulated to fit the exact surface requirements. There are fluorescent lacquers for decal printing, others for printing on cloth, glass, metal and numerous other materials. In addition, fluorescent color comes in oil base mixtures, water-soluble tempera colors, lacquer, luminous flock for appliqué effects, as well as in liquid dyes and sprays.

ENAMELS

Compared to the rapidly drying poster colors we have previously mentioned, enamels usually take a long time to dry, sometimes as much as 7 to 12 hours. Many enamel manufacturers recommend overnight drying. The oven will help set the colors but will not dry them. Why use slow-drying enamels instead of the standard quick-drying poster paints? There are a number of reasons. Enamels have high durability and adhesion qualities. They are excellent for metal signs, glass, wood products, certain plastics, polyethylene bottles, etc. They may, of course, be applied on paper and cardboard as well. Enamels dry with a fair degree of flexibility and produce a very opaque glossy tough coating. Because of their exceptionally smooth consistency, they print beautifully and with a slightly embossed build-up effect. Most enamels are opaque but may be made transparent with the addition of a compatible base. About 800 square feet per gallon is the expected mileage.

Though most enamels are of the "cold" variety, that is, require no baking or firing, there is a baking enamel line made specifically for printing on metal or glass. The required heat exposure is from 275° to 350° F. for a duration of about one hour. This heat treatment does not actually fuse the color into the surface, but sets the color so hard that the print is virtually scratchproof on glass or metal.

ADDITIONAL COLORS

Plastic Color Line

This comprises a group of colors intended for printing on plastics such as acrylics, polystyrene, butyrates, vinyls, heat cured plastics, etc. Actually, there is no one universal color for all plastic

FIG. 71. Screen printing on glassware has become a unique feature of the silk screen process, growing in importance in terms of unmatched quality and diversity. (*Courtesy Eastman Kodak Co.*)

surfaces. The extensive chemical differences among plastic compositions require this bit of caution. Pretest the color on a sample of the actual plastic before you proceed with production. Allow the color to dry and scrupulously test the results for adhesion, as well as for other special requirements.

The plastic color requires lacquer-proof or photo stencils. If the chemist of your paint manufacturer is to be of help to you in formulating a made-to-order color, be sure that you ask him to make the test on the actual plastic to be used on the job. You will find that most process suppliers are very cooperative in the matter of technical assistance on problem jobs. After all, the final results reflect not only on the factors you control, but on the dealer's reputation in supplying you with the necessary materials.

Textile Color Line

The chemistry of textile dyes is quite involved and somewhat outside the sphere of this book. Textile printing by silk screen is an important industry by itself and shares only the principle of the stencil as the sole bond between it and the advertising and industrial phases of the process. However, there are prepared, ready-to-use textile colors on the market today which are at the disposal of the advertising screen processor who is occasionally called upon to handle a job which involves screen printing on cloth. This may include pennants, T-shirts, limited editions of scarves, advertising banners, cloth signs, awnings, cloth novelties, etc.

There are several species of such textile lines available. One is an oil base poly-synthetic paint composition which becomes insoluble upon heat treatment or with time. Heat treatment (when required) consists of subjecting the print for a 5-minute period at 275° F. or for a 2-minute period at 375° F. This is a curing procedure requiring no further chemical processing.

Another type of textile paint of the air-set variety dries within 20 minutes without the need for any heat processing. These paints can be used with almost any type of stencil and have a fair degree of flexibility. Since these colors are for the most part transparent, they are good for light-colored backgrounds only. Available colors are yellow, orange, brilliant green, blue, vermilion, deep red, black and white. Additional colors and shades are achieved by intermixing.

For most textile printing, a fairly coarse mesh (No. 8 or No. 10) is recommended. The supplier of textile colors also provides thinning and thickening agents as well as solvents for cleaning and washing the stencil. In most cases, the results are comparable to

Fig. 72. Textile screen printing is a major industry in its own right quite apart from the advertising phase of the process. (*Courtesy American Crayon Co.*)

printing with dyes, the medium used by the major textile industry. The colors are bright and flexible, and have good holding power to withstand washing, cleaning and exposure. It is important to note that there are variations in the make-up of ready-to-use colors in terms of specific fabrics. These would include canvas, felt, cotton, nylon, burlap, rayon, etc. Consult your dealer for a list of textile colors to suit your needs.

In addition to textile paints, there are also textile screen lacquers.

FIG. 73. An example of a screen-printed commencement cover printed in the classroom with the use of water base screen paint. (*Courtesy High School of Art and Design, New York.*)

These have the advantage of being opaque, and are designed for printing dark-colored materials. They are flexible, cover well, and air-dry in 20 to 30 minutes or heat-set in a matter of seconds. Since these are lacquer base colors, lacquer-proof hand-cut film stencils or photographic stencils are required.

Water Base Poster Paints

In the past, a number of attempts have been made by suppliers to popularize the use of water-soluble (tempera) colors for poster printing. That these attempts have not met with marked success is evidenced by the fact that the use of water-soluble colors is for the most part limited to home or school production. The chief advantages of water base paints are that they are less "messy" than oil or lacquer colors, have no objectionable odor and present no particular fire hazard, and that all it takes to clean the screen is ordinary water. Drawbacks to this color line are that the colors are transparent, are not waterproof, and are not durable.

Whatever the case for or against screen process tempera colors may be, they are available in ready-to-use form and in a variety of very bright hues. You cannot use ordinary artists' poster or showcard colors as substitutes for those manufactured for silk screen. Conventional showcard paints would dry into the mesh of the screen within a matter of minutes and make further printing impossible. The water base colors specifically formulated for silk screen have a built-in plasticizer which retards the drying and produces a smooth flow and good printing consistency. Water base colors can be used with photo or lacquer type stencils only.

Metallic Color Line

Printing with metallic paints has always been considered a feature of screen process. The processor points with pride to the fact that silk screen is the only commercial method for printing an actual metallic paint, in paste form. Other graphic art processes usually print a colorless sizing which requires an additional operation of dusting or "bronzing." This bronze dust is not as bright nor as permanent as a metallic print produced by silk screen in one operation.

Metallic paints are available in gold, silver, copper, as well as an assortment of other color denominations. There are, for instance, about half a dozen different "shades" of gold alone. Although these paints are to be had in paste, ready-to-use form, most processors prefer to buy the powder and vehicle separately and mix the two

Cleaning the glass and setting it into the guides.

Squeegeeing the compound through the screen.

FIG. 74. STEPS IN GLASS ETCHING BY SILK SCREEN USING SCREEN ETCH COMPOUND
(Courtesy McKay Chemical Co., Buffalo)

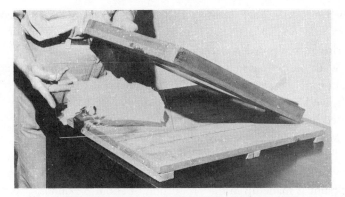

Removing the printed glass from the base.

Washing off the compound.

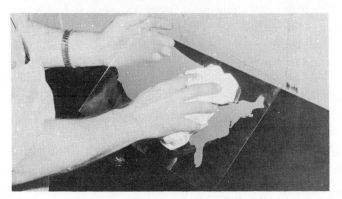

Drying the glass with the etched design.

when needed. The reason for this is that ready-mixed metallic pastes do not keep well when stored, nor are they as bright as a freshly mixed powder-varnish combination.

With the proper make-ready and care in the selection and manipulation of the squeegee, metallic colors lend themselves exceptionally well to a high build-up effect simulating to some degree the raised surface achieved by embossing.

Metallic colors are available for either oil base varnish mixture or lacquer base composition. The powder is the same. The vehicle or varnish is the only difference between the two. In general, metallic paint is made up in the proportion of about 3 pounds of powder to one gallon of vehicle, although this may be varied to suit desired results and conditions. The same ratio of 3 to 1 will apply when mixing a lacquer base metallic color.

Miscellaneous Printing Compounds: Glass Etching Compound

There are two ways whereby the screen process may be employed to produce an etched or frosted design on glassware. And there are ready-made preparations for each. One involves the use of a screening asphaltum. This pitch-like substance, ready prepared to a squeegeeing consistency, is stencilled on the glass. The back and sides of the glass are then protected with asphaltum, so that the only areas open in clear glass are those which are to determine the design.

When the asphaltum print is dry, the glass is totally immersed in an acid bath which affects only those areas which are not covered by the asphaltum. The asphaltum is impervious to the chemical action of the bath. After the acid treatment, the asphaltum resist is dissolved, resulting in a facsimile etched pattern of the stencil. This method can also be used with mirrored surfaces, the result there being that the acid will dissolve away the silvered surface resulting in a mirror design of controlled pattern.

Another method for etching frost effect designs on glass is considerably simpler (Figure 74). It involves the use of a prepared screen compound which is sold under such trade names as "Screen-Etch," "Etch-All," "Glass Etch," etc. The procedure for using this is as follows:

The stencil is prepared in the usual way, and the etching compound is used like paint or any other standard printing medium. The glass to be etched must be thoroughly cleaned with a water-alcohol solution, not crucial as to relative proportion. The etching compound is then screened on the glass and allowed to set for 2 or 3 minutes, after which it is washed off with running water. This stops further chemical action. The glass is then allowed to dry. Glass etching compound works best in room temperatures of 60° to 75° F. In higher temperatures, the "setting" period is shorter. A feature of this etching material is that it is non-injurious to hands with casual contact, although reasonable precaution should be observed and prolonged immersion of the hands in the compound avoided. It is easy to handle and requires no special equipment. The compound can be used with photographic stencils only. It sells for about $3.00 per pound with a companion thinner about $2.00 per pint. When the job is finished, the screen is washed with cold running water, and may be stored away for re-use.

Compounds for Printed Wire and Electro-etching

There are a growing number of ways in which screen process is employed in the electronics industry, some of which have had a revolutionary effect in circuitry and miniaturization. The most prevalent use of silk screen in this area is the employment of conductive silver inks applied by stencils. Metallic paint, like the metal itself, has the property of conducting an electric charge. This means in essence that instead of manually setting fine strands of wire between terminals in an electric circuit, these "wires" are printed through a stencil which deposits a calibrated thickness of metallic paint. The process of "printing" wires by silk screen represents one approach to the problem. There is another phase of this highly technical field which works on the principle of screening a resist compound to produce an etched plate.

Resist compounds. This compound is a fortified black screening lacquer which is resistant to 42-degree Baume Ferric Chloride etchant. After the etching stage, the resist is removed with a companion thinner. Other prepared resist compounds are available for nitric and chromic acid etchants.

Today, screen process is one of the major industrial printing methods for producing printed circuits. When entering upon the domain of chemistry and electronics, specialized knowledge and skills outside the immediate sphere of the average processor's background must be reckoned with. This is within the province of the highly specialized technician in the field. Briefly though incompletely stated, there are two areas here which involve the screen process principle.

Printed circuits. Today, screen process is one of the major production methods for all printed circuits. This in the main involves, as we mentioned before, printing metallic paints which have the property of conducting an electric charge.

Printed coatings and resists. This involves two methods: (1) The plating method (2) The etching method. The *plating method* consists of screening a resist to phenolic laminate or other base material, and depositing a circuit design in unexposed areas. The resist is then removed in an trichloroethylene vapor depressing tank or by similar methods. The *etching method* involves screening a resist upon a copper-clad phenolic insulated panel board. The screen laminate is then immersed into 42-degree Baume Ferric Chloride etchant until the exposed copper has been effected in a trichloroethylene vapor degreasing tank.

ADHESIVE COMPOUNDS

Because of the porous nature of the screen fabric, the screen printing process is commercially adaptable to many other substances besides the traditional paints, lacquers and other printing compounds. We have also seen how the process is used for purposes beyond the sphere of advertising, as, for instance, silk screening with electro-conducting compounds, etching and resist compounds, etc. There is still another industrial use of the process: for the application of commercial and industrial adhesives.

These media fall into two general categories: one, adhesives for gluing and pasting; the other, adhesives for holding tinsel, flocks, etc.

Gluing and Pasting Adhesives

These comprise liquid glues and pastes which serve as a bond between two different surfaces. The most common example would be the application of a coating of glue to cardboard easels to attach them to display cards. Applying glue by stencil methods relieves the operator of the slow and tedious job of using glue pot and brush. Obviously, screening is the more practical and better way of doing the job. This is equally true of similar tasks such as attaching color swatches of cloth, paper, and varied other sample materials used in dealers' catalogs. Commercial glues or pastes are available which have a retarding ingredient to prevent drying into the screen. They are widely used by firms for screening pastes for sample swatching and varied finishing operations.

Appliqué Adhesives

This category includes flocking, tinseling, and beading, which will be discussed in Chapter 13. Suffice it to say here that there are prescribed screening adhesives to be had for a variety of appliqué jobs. These adhesives are individually formulated to adhere well to almost any surface and to serve as an anchorage base for cloth flock, bead, tinsel, and similar appliqué products.

As I have pointed out throughout this book, the resources for products and materials are so abundant that the average processor need not rely on his own incomplete knowledge of chemistry to improvise his own makeshift materials. Get to know the suppliers in your field, is the closing advice for this chapter.

10. COLOR MATCHING AND MIXING

ONE OF THE prime physical requisites of a good color matcher is normal vision. Obviously a person whose vision is poor or who is afflicted with color blindness and cannot differentiate between red and green would be physically unsuited for the job. Another physical requirement associated with the color matcher's job is that he be free from bronchial or skin allergies which may become aggravated by the volatile or chemical properties of the various printing compounds used in the shop.

A good color mixer must also have a well ordered mind with organizational skills to set up and maintain his color department in such a way that everything is in its proper place. In addition, he must cultivate a scientific approach to the problems on hand. He must not be averse to testing, doing research and collecting the technical data of his craft. This does not mean that he must use valuable shop time in purposeless experimentation and improvisations. On the contrary, he will be of greater value to his firm if he keeps abreast of the available resources of the various paint and ink suppliers who service the department.

PREPARATION FOR COLOR MATCHING

Mechanical Aids

Though large ink houses and color laboratories use electronic devices to compare matched colors, the color mixer in the average screen shop relies chiefly on vision to both discern and match colors. He must, however, have the proper lighting facilities. Daylight is

best but it cannot be controlled and therefore proper artificial illumination is important. Fluorescent illumination is preferred because it does not distort color values quite as much as the yellowish
tinge of incandescent lamps.

Stocking Up the Color Department

It would be impractical to keep on hand all of the multitudinous
range of colors that one finds listed in dealers' color catalogs. However, there are certain basic stock colors which should be on hand
at all times in varying quantities. Black and white are the most basic
colors since they are not only used as colors in themselves, but
serve as "mixers" for getting light and dark tones of the other
colors. Figured on a minimal basis of one gallon per color, the
ratio should be about 5 gallons of black and 5 of white to one
gallon of each of the following: lemon yellow, vermilion, turquoise
blue, cerise, ultramarine blue. Theoretically, with these fundamental
colors, most others are achievable through intermixing. Yellow plus
red in the proper proportions will result in an orange. Turquoise
blue intermixed with lemon yellow will produce a bright green,
red and black will give brown, turquoise blue and cerise will produce purple. However, no commercial shop restricts itself to these
few basic colors. Though, theoretically, intermixing will yield an
infinite number of colors and shades, it is more realistic to keep on
hand a number of different kinds of red, a variety of yellows, blues,
greens, etc. In addition, the inventory should include varnishes, reducers and other vehicles, as well as washers and thinners compatible with the various lines of colors used. Some of these lines we
discussed in Chapter 9. They include opaque poster paints, transparent colors, gloss colors, flat colors, lacquers, enamels, fluorescent
colors, metallic colors, etc. The predominance of one particular line
of colors over the others will of course depend upon the nature of
the printing jobs handled. This may be mostly printing on paper
and cardboard, or it may weigh in favor of imprinting on metal,
cloth, plastics or any of the other surfaces discussed elsewhere in
the book. The range and the amount of the inventory of colors will
depend entirely upon the rate of consumption. This bit of advice,
however, may serve as a guide. Do not overstock beyond the antic-

ipated requirements. Storage space is usually at a premium. Let the dealer replenish your basic minimum inventory when you need to do so, and order as your own stock runs low. Within reach of a telephone and rapid transportation facilities for deliveries, your supplier is usually able to service your needs without prolonged delays. Do not let your paint department grow into a morgue of unused colors—a practice which is wasteful, poses a problem in storage, and may constitute a violation of local fire laws. Insurance rates and fire department permits are usually predicated on a maximum number of gallons stipulated in writing. To exceed that constitutes a violation of contract or law.

AIDS IN MATCHING COLORS

Pretest screen. A dab of color finger-smeared on any handy piece of paper does not constitute a reliable color match no matter how closely it may visually approach a given color on the art work. Such a "test" is unreliable because a finger smear is uneven, it does not duplicate the results which will be obtained through the mesh of the screen and the color may not have been applied to the actual stock to be used on the job. All these conditions constitute important factors in the final result. To state this positively, follow these procedures when matching and mixing colors:

1. Match the color as closely as you can and run a sample of it through a test screen set aside for that purpose. This test screen must be of a mesh identical with the full size screen of the actual run.

2. Do the testing on a piece of the actual material which will be used on the job.

3. Allow the screened color swatch to dry thoroughly.

4. Compare the color sample with the corresponding color on the art work. To do this without the optically distorting influences of surrounding colors, cut a small rectangular opening on two separate pieces of paper, forming a window in each. Place one "window" over the color sample and the other "window" over the corresponding color area on the art. You can now compare the

two as you see them through the openings, without visual distractions from surrounding colors.

5. Revise color mixtures and retest them until both colors appear identical.

6. Subject the final color swatch to various tests, which should include desired degree of coverage, adhesion of color to stock, bending, folding and scuffing of print surface. This is of special importance when printing on "difficult" surfaces such as plastics and foils.

7. Check the color periodically while the job is in production.

It would be helpful to review the underlying reasons for each of these suggested seven steps. The reason screen mesh has a bearing on the final match: If the job is to be printed through a very fine mesh, then the color swatch should be printed from a screen of the equivalent mesh size. The thickness of the layer of color influences the exact shade. For this reason it is a good idea to partition off your test screen into several compartments, each with a different mesh screen No. 12, No. 14, No. 16, etc., so that actual mesh conditions are the same for the color test as for the actual job.

The nature of the cardboard (or other printing stock) is a determining factor in the final results achieved. For instance, a particular yellow may seem bright on a non-absorbent gloss-coated board and yet appear as an insipid greenish-yellow on a clay-coated board. To be sure that the conditions of the test are equal to that of the production run, always make the color tests on the actual stock used in production.

When a color dries, it often appears less bright or even of a different cast than in the wet state. A bright chocolate brown, for example, in the wet sample print may, when it dries, take on a chalky and grayish cast. You cannot tell whether you have a good match until the color sample is thoroughly dry.

There are known optical illusions which disturb exact color values in a field of other colors. A gray, for example, placed against an area of black, may appear considerably lighter in value than when viewed on a white ground. In checking a color match, therefore, the surrounding color areas should be masked out. One single way to accomplish this is by viewing both sample and original through identical window openings of a mask.

Many trials and tests may have to be made to match difficult colors. Each time the mixture is revised with the addition of new ingredients, the color must be retested, until finally approved.

The color man's responsibility does not end with the mere visual appearance of the color. That is only one aspect of the task. Another very important responsibility is the mixing of the color. This involves selecting the right line of color, and intermixing it with the prescribed ingredients which influence durability, fastness, flexibility, adhesion, degree of opacity, gloss, etc. A color may be perfectly matched but may flake off after it is dry. Or it may be bright when freshly printed but may fade rapidly upon prolonged atmospheric exposure. It is for these reasons that on jobs when adhesion, fastness or some other special factor is particularly important, the color man must re-examine his color swatches after they have been drying for some time before subjecting the color to further tests to determine its fitness for the exacting demands of the job on hand.

While the job is in production, especially at the beginning of the run, it is the job of the color man to continue to check results. Colors usually do not change in the screen, but they may be somewhat affected by variations in squeegee pressure, escape of certain volatile ingredients, and viscosity changes. In order to sustain standard color uniformity it is a good trade practice to set aside a few strike-off "master" sheets to be referred to as the standard during the entire course of production.

As we have seen, the color man's responsibility is twofold. One is the visual matching of color to conform to the art, the other is the preparation of the bulk batch of color for the actual printing. Both phases are obviously interrelated, as they involve choosing a right line to start with, mixing the color with the prescribed ingredients, etc. In essence, the task of mixing the color starts off with estimating the amount needed for the job. As we have learned, this varies with the size of the run, the type of color used, the printing area, the mesh of the screen, the type and surface of the stock, etc. The range of color consumption is therefore broad—400 to 1200 square feet of coverage per gallon. The experienced color man is usually able to estimate the anticipated consumption with a fair degree of accuracy. Since it would be rather time-consuming to rematch a difficult color shade should a shortage arise during the printing, it is wise to go a little beyond the estimate, even if it means that some color is left over after the job is completed. What happens to the left-over batches of color from various jobs? This will be the subject of the next paragraph.

Each left-over color should be placed back in a can, covered, and identified with a label. This label should show the following: A swatch test of the color, the date on which the color was mixed, the line or special formula of ingredients, the name of the job or client, etc. In the course of daily production, many colors thus accumulate

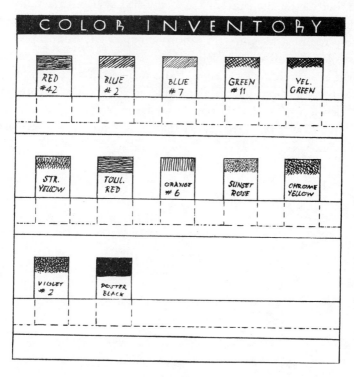

FIG. 75. Suggestion for movable card index system to serve as a visual guide to inventory of paints on hand.

and are added to the inventory. A chaotic and wasteful condition is perpetuated unless some effective system of identification is established. The left-overs, properly identified, are saved rather than discarded for two reasons. First, to be readily available in the event of a rerun at some future time. Second, to be used as one of the basic starting colors for future jobs. Good husbandry of the paint department will keep the inventory down to a practical minimum and keep the shelves free from "dead wood" of heterogeneous unidentified mixtures.

Inventory keeping must be systematic. One way to help accomplish this is to keep a chart such as shown in Figure 75. Other ways may be devised which are equally good or better. The important thing is not so much emphasis on any particular system initiated, but the maintenance of the established system. In a well run paint department, an accurate record of all the colors is kept, visibly recorded by sample, quantity, mixture, etc. This applies to new colors as well as to the left-overs.

The resourceful color man will also maintain a well kept file of dealers' color charts and catalogs indexed for ready reference. He will develop a friendly personal relationship with his suppliers and feel free to call on them for technical assistance on special color problems.

11. FACTS ON PAPER, BOARD AND OTHER PRINTING SURFACES

IN VIEW OF the great variety of printing surfaces which are screened today, it would be a herculean task to catalog them all here. Indeed, such an encyclopedic record of materials classified as to size, weight and uses would be more impressive than useful. Manufacturers and dealers of such materials spare no expense in time and money to issue lavish brochures of their current lines. Even these go into obsolescence rapidly, and revised editions are redistributed with new colors, new sizes, new prices and other pertinent particulars.

There was a time when screen printing was associated mostly with paper and cardboard. That no longer is true today. Paper and board surfaces represent only one category of printing surfaces. Other categories include woods, glass, metal, rubber, leather and a variety of plastic materials, used in display, fabrication, and diverse industrial applications. Obviously these could not all be listed here. To give up all attempts at cataloging any of these as hopeless, however, because they cannot all be adequately treated within the limited space of one chapter, would arbitrarily cancel the author's obligations to the reader. With your indulgence, therefore, I shall limit my survey to cardboard and paper since these are of greatest interest to the processors of posters, displays, and the more traditional point-of-sale advertising.

CARDBOARD

Under this head is included cardboard of varying thicknesses, used primarily by poster and display printers. There are in the main three basic types of display board stock: (1) clay coated (2) patent coated (3) lined.

Clay coated board. This stock derives its name from a smooth coating of a white clay substance which covers the surface of stock. Clay coated board comes in just about any caliper or "point." The features of this particular stock are the high degree of whiteness of the coating and the smooth surface. There are no discernible hills or valleys which characterize the fibrous pulp matter which goes into the making of the board. Clay coated board, because of its smooth clean surface, is fine for photographic halftone printing, as well as for routine printing jobs. It is not recommended for displays which are to be die cut with complicated scoring or folding because clay coated board has a tendency to crack somewhat at the point of deep scores or tight folds.

Patent coated board. This is similar to clay board stock but both sides of the board are covered with a "liner." This is a smooth well-finished sheet of paper, superior in quality to the layers of paper within the board itself. This paper liner serves not only as an excellent printing surface but acts as a "hinge" when the board is cut, scored or crease-folded in the die cutting operation. Patent coated boards are obtainable in various colors as well as the standard white and in different thicknesses.

Lined board. This, like the patent coated board, is stock which has a lining of paper, usually on both sides. The inside or bulk of the cardboard is made of a cheaper material, such as newsboard, which is somewhat rough. Though the liner covers some of the roughness, it does not completely obliterate the hills and valleys. Lined board, though not of a superior surface quality, is, however, very acceptable for die cutting because the liner acts as a hinge. It is available in color as well as in metallic foils such as gold and silver.

MISCELLANEOUS PRINTING STOCKS

Newsboard. This is a cheap pulp stock characterized by a somewhat uneven and flecked surface texture. It is grayish in color and

FIG. 76. Sturdy and well-designed floor stand display screen printed on corrugated board to withstand the weight of the actual product advertised. (*Courtesy Poster Products, Inc., Chicago.*)

comparatively inexpensive. This gray color may be obliterated by screening with opaque paint, but it may take more than one color to do an effective coating job, especially if the paint is of light value, such as yellow, white, or pastel shades. Newsboard is used for construction elements of a display, such as concealed box easels, supporting struts or other construction units hidden from view.

Chipboard. This is similar to newsboard but is inferior to it. The surface is rougher and the flakes or wood chips from which it derives its name, are more pronounced.

Jute board. This is a very tough resinous board, usually brown in color, used principally in easels and struts for displays. It has strong fibrous qualities which make it ideal for folding and creasing.

Corrugated board. This is a popular board, which though light in weight, is very strong and weight-sustaining. It is used mostly for floor stand displays, counter stands and shipping containers. Unlike other boards, corrugated stock comes in two thicknesses only: "B" flute, which is about ⅛″ thick, and "A" flute, which is twice the thickness. Available in standard sheet sizes of 50″ x 76″, it can be die cut but cannot be cut-scored. It takes an excellent fold or crease.

Cover stock. This is a good quality strong fibered white material representing a cross between paper and board. It is characterized by a good printing surface and substantial bending and folding properties. It is available in different weights, colors and sizes.

Kromekote. This is a marble-smooth stock, extremely white and bright. Because of its relatively high cost, it is reserved only for the finest printing jobs and fine dot halftone. Though it is really a paper rather than a board, it can be mounted on any desired thickness. It is the "Tiffany" of printing surfaces.

Showcard board. This comes in a wide array of colors including metallics and woodgrain design. One manufacturer lists more than 30 different colors, ranging from subtle pastels to vivid hues and shades. It is available in a standard size of 28″ x 44″ in 14 ply (48 point).

Weatherproof board. This is a white surfaced patent coated stock made for exterior use. This weatherproof property is due to an impregnated waterproof additive introduced into the manufacture of the board at the mill. Stock thicknesses are 21 to 80 point in a large variety of sizes. It is also available in paper.

Metallic surfaces. These are lustrous foil papers in a wide assortment of metallic colors, in addition to the traditional gold and silver. The collection includes smooth, highly polished surfaces, as well as a veritable gallery of embossed designs and patterns. Standard sheet size is 20″ x 26″ but it is also to be had in stock size rolls 26″ wide and cut to any required length.

Also popular today are highly polished metallic plastic sheets in cellulose acetate, butyrate, polystyrene, mylar and other plastic compositions. Great caution must be exercised in screening on such diverse plastic surfaces, to assure adhesion of color to the printing surface. A paint or lacquer that works on one plastic is not necessarily compatible for all plastics. Pre-run proofs, allowed to dry and tested for adhesion, should always precede actual production.

Fluorescent Sheets. These are smooth surfaced papers coated in the standard vivid fluorescent paints. They are also available with an adhesive back. Fluorescent sheets are obtainable in waterproof vinyl plastic as well as paper.

Velour paper. This is a plush-like paper made with precision-cut flock. Standard sheet size is 20" x 26½", though in large quantities, 40" stock, in any of about 15 colors, can be made to order. It is available in flat or design-embossed surfaces.

Flint papers. These are highly polished sheets in a bright array of colors. They are used principally for expensive wrappings.

General Notes on Paper and Board

The thickness of board is measured by point or ply. A *point* is the equivalent of 1/1000 of an inch. A piece of stock 10 points in thickness would measure 1/100 of an inch. 50 pt. stock would measure 1/20 of an inch, a piece of stock 100 points in thickness would measure 1/10 of an inch, etc.

Ply is the unit of measure of thickness of the lighter weight stock. To convert ply to point, multiply the ply number by 3 and add 6. For instance: To convert 14 ply into its point equivalent, multiply 14 x 3 which is 42, then add 6, bringing the total to 42 plus 6, or 48 point.

When ordering stock, thought must be given to the direction of the grain. To determine which way the grain is running, tear a piece of the stock at both dimensions. The stock will tear more easily along the grain side. It will tear with greater resistance against the grain. Grain direction is important in die cutting, as well as in poster and display work where the stock is made to stand on end. In a 14″ x 22″ upright sign, the grain should run the 22″ way. If the grain were to run the 14″ way, there would be a growing tendency on the part of the sign to warp or droop over like a tree bent by a strong wind.

All paper and board are subject to expansion or contraction with fluctuating weather conditions. This is especially true of "green" stock. By that is meant board, especially of the lined variety, which is fresh from the mill or the mounter and has not as yet had sufficient time to dry or season. Unseasoned lined stock often shows considerable shrinkage, thus affecting the alignment of colors in close register multicolor printing. To offset this condition, it is advisable to air the cards in open racks or send them through the drying oven before printing. This is referred to as "seasoning" the stock.

Paper is not ordered by point size as cardboard is. The thickness of paper is measured in terms of *pound*, as 60 lb., 80 lb., 100 lb., etc. This is determined by the weight in pounds of a ream of paper cut to standard size. The standard size which is the basis for the weight, varies with different types of paper. For instance, the basic size of book papers (the most commonly used in screen process) is 25″ x 38″. It is upon this basic size in a ream (500 sheets) quantity that the basic weight is calculated. Thus a "70 lb." basic weight paper means that 500 sheets of it, cut to sheet size of 25″ x 38″, would weigh 70 lbs. The 500-sheet weights of sizes other than the basic size vary in proportion to the area. This means that you can get a 35″ x 45″ or other size in 70 lb. (or any other weight) but that the weight is still determined on the standard 25″ x 38″ size. Weights of paper vary from 30 lb. to 120 lb.—the greater the weight, the thicker the paper. Thus a sheet of 120 lb. paper is four times the thickness of a sheet of 30 lb. paper.

As in cardboard, paper has a definite grain, but this is not crucial as in cardboard stock. The grain is determined by the direction of the paper parallel to its forward movement on the paper machine. Normally, the majority of fibres lie parallel to the machine direction. Cross direction or cross grain is the direction of the paper at right angles to the paper machine. Generally, the strength of the sheet is greater *across* than with the grain. .

Paper is available in coated, antique, eggshell, plate, vellum and a variety of decorative finishes. A well maintained filing system with catalogued samples of dealer brochures of paper, card and a variety of other printing surfaces is a "must" in every well organized screen shop.

12. DECALCOMANIAS: HOW TO PRINT THEM, HOW TO USE THEM

PRINCIPLE OF THE DECALCOMANIA

THE DECAL (short for decalcomania) is a transfer print made to adhere to that kind of surface upon which it is impossible or impractical to print directly. Examples are trade marks or lettering on machinery, lettering on vehicles, decorative designs on furniture, lettering on multiple windows, etc. The decal design is printed by silk screen on a sheet of special gum-surfaced paper manufactured for that purpose. The print is then transferred by direct contact from the paper to any surface, flat or curved. The decal print conforms to any surface to which it is applied.

TYPES OF DECAL PAPER

There are two types, *simplex* or single transfer slide-off, and *duplex* or double transfer paper, each having a distinct use in the trade.

Simplex is a specially prepared paper which has been coated with an invisible water-soluble dextrine adhesive film which carries the print. The simplex decal is made for application to glass, ceramics, and most paint surfaces.

Duplex or double transfer paper is recommended for outdoor applications where resistance to exposure is important. In application, the tissue paper carrying the design is peeled from the backing sheet. After removal face down, the tissue is dampened and removed. It is usually applied to a tacky, varnished surface.

Though there are two types of decal paper, there are actually four different types of decals:

1. Slide-off type. The printed image (face up) in this type slides off the paper backing sheet onto the surface to be decorated.

2. Face-down type. This decal is printed in reverse, so that to see the finished or unfinished decal during production, the sheet must be held up to the light and read through the paper backing sheet. In this type, the decal, when fully completed, shows only the finishing coating and the backing sheet. The design is underneath. This decal is transferred paint side down (paper side up) to the surface which is to carry the design. The paper backing sheet is then slid off, leaving the decal adhering to the surface.

3. Duplex or varnish type. This is printed on a special paper which is really composed of two papers, a tissue paper and an opaque heavy paper. It is printed always face down. A coat of tacky varnish is necessary for adhesion.

4. Face-up type. This is similar to the slide-off type and is mostly used for the inside of glass windows. Although this decal is printed as a slide-off decal, it is transferred to the *inside* of a store window but is viewed from the outside reading the right way.

METHODS OF USING DECALS

How to Print Simplex Single Transfer Decals

Let us suppose that you want to produce a decal design with the following specifications: a yellow circle 6″ in diameter on which the lettering "Give to the Red Cross" appears in red. You cut decal paper a little larger than the 6″ circle area. In preparing stencils for this job, you first make a stencil for a circle of clear decal lacquer 6⅛″ in diameter. This base coating of clear lacquer, slightly larger than the 6″ yellow circle shown on the art work, forms an invisible film on which the subsequent colors are later printed. It is the invisible base which acts as a transfer medium, keeping the design intact until it is safely transferred to the surface which is to receive the design. This clear lacquer as well as all subsequent prints are screened on the gummed side of the decal paper.

When the coating of clear lacquer is screened and allowed to dry, prepare the stencil for the 6″ yellow circle. This is printed to register within the 6⅛″ circle of lacquer. Then, when that is dry, print the red, registered properly. If the registering and feeding have been done carefully, you should now have a 6″ solid yellow circle, printed on a 6⅛″ lacquer area, showing a slight overdraw all around. When the red is dry, overprint another coat of lacquer (using the previous 6⅛″ circle stencil). In other words, you have followed your regular printing procedure except that you have sandwiched your print between two coats of transparent lacquer, a base coat and a finishing coat.

The decal you have just made is good for application to walls, wooden doors, machinery and other solid surfaces.

How to Transfer Simplex Slide-off Decals

Immerse the decal in a pan filled with water. Allow the decal to soak for 20 to 30 seconds. What happens is that the water is absorbed through the underside of the paper (non-paint side) until the water-soluble gum surface coating is reached. Now, lift the dripping wet paper and place it, print side facing you, in position on the wall or whatever surface the design is to be applied to. Then very carefully slide the paper out from underneath. Then, using the discarded wet paper as a flattening surface, smooth out the decal so that no air bubbles or wrinkles are evident. Once the water dries out, the decal design will appear as if it were actually printed on the surface to which it has adhered.

How to Transfer Duplex or Double Transfer Decals

Wipe the backing sheet with a cloth soaked with water, but not dripping wet. Then brush on a thin coat of special adhesive decal varnish to the face of the decal. Next, wait 10 minutes or so for the adhesive to become tacky. In the meantime, clean the surface to which the decal is to be applied, being sure to free it from all grease, dirt or dust. Then wet this surface with water. Now, carefully place the decal in position (print side down) and squeegee it with either a piece of cardboard, window wiper or rubber squeegee, working from the center out toward the edge. Then remove the initial backing paper carefully, so as not to disturb the second sheet of paper. Wash the adhered and dried decal with water to remove all traces of adhesive.

How To Use the Duplex Face-down type

If the decal is of very large dimensions, it becomes difficult, in the act of transferring it, to deftly slip away the backing paper. For large size work, therefore, the face-down type is used. This decal is printed in reverse, that is, the painted surface cannot be seen as it is printed. In order to see the finished or as yet unfinished decal as it progresses, the sheet must be held up to the light and read through the backing paper. Because the decal is printed in reverse order or sequence, the background color is printed last. This type of decal is applied with the paint side down. The paper backing sheet is merely lifted off leaving the decal adhering to the object.

FOUR POINTS TO REMEMBER IN HANDLING DECALS

1. Use only special paints or lacquers manufactured specifically for decal printing. Do not use standard poster colors as they may not be flexible enough.

2. Keep the decal blank sheets of unprinted paper well covered when stored away. Decal papers, because of their gum coating, have a tendency to curl when exposed to changing weather conditions. Well equipped decal printing establishments use humidifiers and air conditioning systems to assure stability and flatness of decal papers and as an aid in color registration controls.

3. Use a stencil technique to suit the type of printing medium. For instance, in using decal lacquers, you cannot use a hand-cut lacquer stencil, as the stencil will dissolve in printing. A photo stencil or water base cut film will be, of course, right for lacquer or paint.

4. Meticulous cleanliness is necessary in handling decals, both in printing and transferring them. Any foreign matter in the decal will result in a pimple or blemish in the image-film. Also, unless the surface is thoroughly clean, free from dust, grease or oil, the adhesion of the decal will be imperfect.

To insure against sticking or offsetting when decals are packed for shipment or storage, it is good policy always to insert individual slip sheets between each pair of adjoining prints.

13. FLOCK, TINSEL AND OTHER APPLIQUÉ MATERIALS

THE USE OF the screen process in the application of adhesives for appliqué work has evolved into a separate branch of the industry, quite apart from that which deals with color printing for advertising. There are a number of popular appliqué products, among them being flock, tinsel, and beads. There are others, but the materials, equipment and procedures are similar enough to be encompassed in the general description which follows.

FLOCK

Flock is a term used to describe finely cut cloth fibres which are thrown, dusted or scattered onto a gummy surface. When the adhesive dries, the flock material remains anchored, simulating the effect of suede, velour, and other cloth textures. The excess flock is then blown or shaken off. Flocking is extensively used in the

FIG. 77. Example of a typical school pennant with a flocked screen printed design. (*Courtesy High School of Art and Design, New York.*)

application of lettering or designs on T-shirts, pillow covers, emblems, pennants, textile prints, and advertising novelties. Flock comes in a wide variety of cloth fibres, such as wool, rayon, nylon, cotton and silk; and in varying lengths of cloth fibres. It is also produced in a generous assortment of pastel colors, brilliant spectrum colors, gold and silver, and even in fluorescent and lustrous phosphorescent colors. Flock material is sold by the pound and is stocked in ½ mm, 1 mm and 1½ mm lengths but can be made up to any required length or color to correspond to the needs of the job on hand.

TINSEL

The flittering sparkle effects you see on greeting cards are achieved with tinsel products applied to a tacky surface. This sparkle dust may be made of any one of a number of different products, depending upon the effect required. Here are some:

Diamond dust. This is a clear transparent material which produces a glittering highlight reflection. It is frequently seen on sign cards and greeting cards. It is sold in coarse, medium, fine or extra fine flakes and is sold by the pound or drum.

Silver glass tinsel. This is a brilliant and highly reflective glass mirror substance ground or cut into fine particles.

Colored glass tinsel. These are brilliantly dye-coated glass mirrors, cut very fine and put up in a wide range of colors.

Cellophane spangles. This is a lightweight lustrous sparkle dust available in white as well as in different colors.

Mother of pearl flakes. This is a crushed mother of pearl dust dyed in a generous assortment of pastel colors.

Non-tarnishable aluminum tinsel. Though the most popular color is a lustrous, mirror-like silver, non-tarnishable aluminum tinsel is also produced in blue, red, green, chartreuse, pink and cerise. Not only is there an assortment in size of the minute flakes, but in the shapes as well, as, for instance, hexagons, squares, triangles, etc.

METHOD OF APPLYING FLOCKED PRODUCTS

The adhesive compound is printed through the conventional stencil onto the surface which is to receive the flock. A fairly coarse mesh screen is recommended to assure a substantial deposit of the adhesive. There is no limit as to the kind of surface for flocking. It may be paper, cloth, metal, glass, fabric, etc. However, the particular adhesive used must be appropriate to the surface.

After the adhesive is screened, the print is ready to receive the flock. This may be done in any one of different ways. The simplest (though not very efficient for large runs) is to scatter the dust onto the tacky surface manually, using a trough or wide mesh flour sieve. This print is then shaken vigorously and then allowed to dry for several hours. The length of drying time is determined by the nature of the adhesive as well as the nature of the surface to which it is applied.

Another method involves the use of a flock gun with a large receptacle (Figure 78). If you use this method, you will fill the

FIG. 78. Flock gun.

FIG. 79. A see-saw rocking tray useful in applying flock and tinsel material. (*Courtesy Advance Process Supply Co.*)

receptacle ¾ full with flock. Adjust air pressure to about 30–35 pounds. Aim the flock gun at the wet print. The force of the air pressure will shoot the flock out of the nozzle and onto the wet adhesive area. Shake off the excess flock and allow the print to dry.

Another method of applying the flock is to employ a vibrating mechanism, which can be purchased for that purpose. This consists of a motor-driven platform which, agitated by a cam, keeps the platform in continuous vibration. The adhesive wet print is placed on the platform and then, either by hand methods or by gun, the flock is directed over the wet surface. The vibrating action of the platform will shake the dust well into the receiving surface and consequently make for a good bond between the two.

Other mechanical devices include a turntable with a revolving platform. The flock by centrifugal force distributes itself well over the adhesive to which it is applied. Another simple jig consists of a see-saw box in which both flock and print are rocked. This motion distributes the flock over the wet surface of the print (Figure 79).

So far we have discussed manual and mechanical flocking techniques. There is still another, used widely by firms which are set up for large volume industrial flocking. This system works on an entirely different principle, based on the phenomenon of static electricity. In essence, an electrostatic condition is set up whereby the flock material is charged with electrical energy, and is irresistibly drawn to the adhesive surface. This is pretty much the same phenomenon which occurs when a haircomb attracts small bits of paper after it is rubbed over a furry surface.

Elaborate flocking units based on the electrostatic principle, one of which is shown in Figure 80, are on the market; these are designed to keep up with the fast production pace of the industry. Such units not only apply the flock automatically, but draw off the surplus as well. This mechanizes an operation which by hand is comparatively slow and messy. It reduces waste to a minimum and produces a better and more uniform job. Electrostatic units are available for unit piece printing, as well as continuous yardage from a roll or bolt. In essence, the cycle is as follows:

The adhesive is applied to the material which is to be flocked by fast automatic screen presses. When it leaves the press, the material travels by conveyer belt and enters the enclosed flocking zone. There it is electrostatically flocked and electrostatically pre-cleaned. The flocked material passes the zone where it is pneumatically

FIG. 80. Automatic flocking machine used by industrial flockers. (*Courtesy American Screen Process Equipment Co.*)

cleaned, removing all surplus unadhered flock. The finished material is then ejected onto a conveyor belt, on which it is transported for drying.

14. PRINTING ON CYLINDRICAL AND UNUSUAL SURFACES

THOUGH screen process had its origin as a "flat surface" printing method, it has now branched out into a major industrial process for printing on curved surfaces and three-dimensional products of all shapes. Indeed, the application of silk screen to three-dimensional surfaces is so widespread that this tributary of the process is surpassing in total volume the screening business of flat surface printing in the advertising and display field. In addition to cylindrical, spherical, convex, and concave surfaces, silk screen is widely used for printing on such fabricated materials as table tops, toys, boxes, ceramic tiles, and the like. The basic silk screen principle remains the same but the make-ready, paint, and special equipment are adjusted to the job on hand.

CYLINDRICAL SURFACES

Most screening on round surfaces is accomplished with a flat stencil. The stencil rests directly on the curvature or crest of the cylindrical surface to be screened, which in turn rotates on ball-bearing rolling pins. The screen is in contact with the cylindrical surface of the object. As the screen is moved sideways, it turns the object with it, thus rotating it on the pins. This is no doubt an over-simplification of the procedure, but it helps to differentiate the action of printing on a rotating surface from that on a stable flat surface.

The simplest of the cylindrical printing units is hardly more than a jig. The most elaborate represents a complex automatic piece of equipment with a production capacity of thousands of impressions per hour.

The "Sparky" jig, a trade name for one of several simple units, is shown in Figure 81. In operation, the cylindrical object is cradled

FIG. 81. The "Sparky" jig, a simple device for screening on round objects.

beneath the screen and is revolved beneath it. The squeegee itself remains stationary, but the screen is moved on its tracks from side to side, delivering the impression by momentary contact. This unit is manually operated, inexpensive, and comes in several models, depending upon the size and circumference of the object to be printed. The "Streamliner," another trade-named unit, is shown in Figure 82.

Other manufacturers produce a full array of units from foot-controlled, semi-automatic units costing about $1000 to high speed completely automatic machines engineered to cost many thousands of dollars, depending upon the complexity of the operation.

Space does not permit here to explain or even show the wide variety of screening units now available for cylindrical printing.

FIG. 82. The "Streamliner," a screening set-up for printing on large cylindrical objects. (*Courtesy Atlas Silk Screen Supply Co.*)

Suffice it here to say that the problem of screening on round surfaces has been a challenge successfully met by machine engineers and that they have come up with equipment to fit practically every industrial need. By way of illustrating the wide range of equipment, there is the "Sparky" jig, a simple piece of inexpensive equipment, while Figure 82 shows a high speed unit which is a finely engineered piece of completely automatic equipment with a capacity of 2000 impressions per hour. Multicolor registration is carried out by gears, which rotate the object to be printed in synchronization with frame movement.

In addition to round or cylindrical objects, there is automatic equipment available for all types of cone-shaped objects. This, as well as the previously mentioned units, allows for accurate registra-

FIG. 83. Fully automatic turret printer designed for high-speed screening on cylinders. It features a multicolor registration device and an automatic inflating device for soft wall plastic containers. (*Courtesy American Screen Process Equipment Co.*)

tion and standards of printing which meet the highest level of craftsmanship.

Continuous Roll Printing

Gift wrapping papers in continuous rolls are screen printed with a patented machine designed for the purpose. A 800-yard roll of paper is fed into a machine, printed, dried and rerolled in one continuous operation, at a speed of about 90 feet per minute or about

1600 impressions per hour. This is done with an ingeniously engineered screen cylinder of stainless steel wire cloth, with the squeegee operating internally. It is necessary, as in all continuous roll printing, to print skip repeats. This is done in exact register so that the gaps are filled in unbroken design. Mechanical clips on the conveyer grasp the sheet as it leaves the printing unit and lead it to the dryer. Printing from a cylindrical screen in continuous rolls is not as yet extensively used, but is a major interest of a number of enterprising firms who are specifically set up for this type of production.

Flocking, too, is produced by automatic continuous roll screen presses similar to the operation of the paper screening machine.

HIGH BUILD-UP FLATWARE SCREENING UNITS

We have said that screening is done on industrial tiles, boxes, and other fabricated and three-dimensional objects. Just as there are machines of varying degrees of automation for printing on cylindrical and cone-shaped objects, there are professional printing units available for flatware and odd-shaped objects. For instance, there is even an automatic unit especially designed for screening on plates and saucers. The "Dubuit" printer, a press designed for industrial printing, has a production speed of over 1000 objects an hour and prints plates up to 16″ in diameter. The screen for printing the center part of the plate is mounted on a special frame and a patented squeegee passes over the center while another operation squeegees the raised embankment of the plate.

In addition, there are units available for glass, metal and wood flatware.

MISCELLANEOUS SURFACES AND SHAPES

Where screening is geared to mass production, no "makeshift" jig will suffice. When an entire factory is blueprinted to screen bottles, containers, or some other similar industrial product, it is natural that only the most efficient equipment custom built for the purpose be employed.

There are occasions, however, when the average screen printer requires a "jig" for printing on some odd surface such as a limited edition of T-shirts, fabricated boxes, lamp bases, or other odds and ends which to him represent a departure from his normal preoccupation with screening on poster paper and board. In most cases, personal ingenuity and pride in craftsmanship will prompt the operator to improvise his own jigs. But he can get help in this direction from his local silk screen suppliers, some of whom maintain a department for this purpose.

A comparatively simple problem such as the following will suggest the direction of improvisation. Suppose you had to silk screen on a quantity of ½"-high wood panels. Two ways suggest themselves for meeting this problem. One is to raise the hinges so that the screen is elevated over the printing base, the same height as the thickness of the object to be printed. To assure an even riding surface for the squeegee as it passes over the screen during printing, it will be necessary to glue or nail ½" strips of wood or layers of board all around the object to be printed as it rests in register on the printing base (Figure 84).

Another way is to cut out a depressed area or recess in the printing table itself into which the object to be printed is lowered in register. In this case, the frame hinges need not be elevated.

FIG. 84. Simple jigs can be bought or improvised to accommodate fabricated and three-dimensional objects. (*Courtesy Advance Process Supply Co.*)

FIG. 85. Very effective applications of designs on commercial containers screened by machines with a special paint which requires no firing. (*Courtesy Wornow Process Paint Co. and Curtis, Sarver and Witzerman, Inc., Los Angeles.*)

In the same manner, other jigs may be improvised to print with a special screen, contour-shaped to fit the varying surfaces of the object to be decorated. This may call for considerable dexterity in molding the screen to correspond to the shape of the object. It would be impossible and needless here to attempt to anticipate the exigencies arising out of the unique "problem" jobs which occasionally drift into the average screen shop. A lathe, jig saw, hand tools, and native ingenuity will suggest ways and means of doing the job. That failing, or when the stakes are too high, call on the services of your screen process supplier.

15. TEXTILE AND WALLPAPER PRINTING

SCREEN PRINTING on textiles and on wallpaper is done in two principal ways: In one method, on individual sheets, each piece is fed into position on either a stationary bed or a moving belt. The other way involves printing in bolts or rolls on very long, specially constructed tables. Our prime interest in this chapter will be the first category, namely, handling the printing material as an individual unit or sheet. In large scale commercial textile or wallpaper printing, two distinct industries in themselves, the continuous bolt method is used. These industries, however, are so highly specialized in techniques that they are not within the scope of this book. In commercial textile printing from the bolt, for instance, the stencils are different from those used in poster printing. The method of registration is different, and so are the drying, the squeegeeing, and especially the color mixing. In fact, the only thing this branch of the process has in common with poster printing is that it shares the basic principle of the stencil. Wallpaper printing from rolls, too, has become so highly specialized as to deserve better treatment than we can give it here in the space of one chapter. We shall, therefore, confine ourselves here to the method of screening piece or unit textile and wallpaper and only briefly touch on general information relative to bolt or roll printing.

PAINT

Paint will vary with the nature of the material. Paint companies formulate colors for a large category of materials, which include wearing apparel, towels, tablecloths, scarves, and a great variety of textile novelties. The colors, which one manufacturer lists as "Tex-dyes," are pigment emulsions in concentrated pastes to be used in combination with a color carrier, called "Texdye Extender." These colors have good wash fastness and resistance to dry cleaning when properly treated. "Treatment" consists of drying and curing. Printed fabrics, after drying thoroughly to be free from residual solvents, must be subjected to heat. The heat brings about chemical reaction or "cure," creating a permanent bond between color and fabric. The curing cycle varies from 5 minutes at 260° F. to 1 minute at 375° F. depending upon the fabric used.

Another line of textile colors is formulated on the principle of cotton and absorbent fabrics which requires no heat treatment; any type of cut film or photo stencil may be used. This is a series of colors sold as "air-set" textile colors. These paints dry within 20 to 30 minutes without heat processing, although heat may be used to hasten the drying and add to the fastness and washability of the fabric.

Another line of textile colors is formulated on the principle of water base and oil emulsion. These, when heat treated, become durable and fast. The colors must be used with a companion ex-tender in varying proportions. The final color depth and brilliance will depend upon the proportions used and the thoroughness of the mix. The colors print with a transparent and dye-like effect, and printing one color over another produces additional tones. These colors, being transparent, are limited to white or light-colored fabrics.

There are other paints and lacquers for felt, canvas, denim, and a variety of other fabrics too numerous to mention here. Suffice it to say that suppliers have printing media available for specific uses. The textile screening industry as a whole, however, does not always rely on these ready-to-use colors; instead, they often prefer to mix their own developed dye formulations, as well as discharge or acid colors which may be used on any colored background, including black. They also employ repitigen or caustic colors which are tub fast and very brilliant. Because of the caustic nature of these dyes, the life of the stencil is comparatively short. The textile industry also uses vat colors, which are extremely fast and laundry-proof.

Screen process paints used in wallpaper printing do not have as many subsidiary lines as those used in textile printing. Basically, there are three categories of wallpaper printing compounds: oil base colors, which are essentially the same as those used in poster printing, water base emulsion colors and lacquers. In each case, the color must be flexible to allow for rolling the paper, permanently and chemically unresponsive to active penetration of paste or other adhesive materials used in pasting, and waterproof.

STENCILS

The type of piece goods printing associated with screening T-shirts, scarves, novelty pillow cases, felt banners, etc. requires no special method other than that used in the general poster field. However, the situation is different in large scale textile printing of dress fabrics, shirting, towel and tablecloth screening, etc. The industrial use of caustic dyestuff requires a stencil that will withstand the caustic ingredients in the dye. One way such stencils are prepared is as follows:

The screen is coated with a thin solution of dextrine. Then the design is painted in with a water-soluble resist material such as tusche. When the resist is dry, a bakelite varnish filler is scraped on the upper side of the screen on which the resist design has been painted. After the varnish dries, both sides of the screen are washed to remove the dextrine and the resist. Next, the screen is reinforced from the back by a coating of bakelite varnish, which is immediately removed from the topside of the open mesh by a wash of turpentine.

Hand-cut stencil films and specially treated photo stencils are also used, but no one stencil method is as yet permanently impervious to the continued biting action of the acid in the dyestuff. Repeated stencils must be available for very large runs, or stencils must be inspected and touched up periodically for extended use.

In wallpaper work, no such stencil problem exists. Since the paints are more or less the same as for poster and display printing, the stencils likewise are the conventional type—tusche, hand-cut film and photographic.

MAKE-READY

In piece goods or sheet printing, the material to be printed is registered into the printing guides the same as in poster printing. In screening textiles, a No. 8 or No. 6, or even coarser mesh is used to permit a full flow-through of color for better penetration. The printing base may be either felt, sponge rubber, cotton padding or a hard surface, depending upon the fabric to be printed. For plushy pennant material, for instance, a soft cushioning padding on the printing base will permit a fuller and better application of color. In other fabrics, especially very flexible material, a smooth hard base may be best. To avoid the shift of material during the passing of the squeegee, and to assure good registration in multi-color work, a pressure-sensitive table wax is often used to hold the piece goods in register. This wax-like adhesive may also be used as an applicator to the cardboard to which each fabric is temporarily mounted. The mount, cardboard and all, is then fed into the guides. Each sheet of material will have its own cardboard. After printing is completed in all colors, the fabric is easily stripped off and the cardboard may be re-used. Other systems involve the use of a cloth-padded base, onto which the fabric to be printed is tacked or pinned into position for each print.

Registration of wallpaper sheets is done in the conventional manner of poster printing. Wallpaper designs come in several categories. One is scenic work. This is a mural-like scene or illustrated background, a favorite among interior decorators of homes and industrial establishments. A "scenic" is printed in a number of large sheets, and it takes several sheets, pasted individually on the wall in proper sequence, to give the effect of a continuous hand-painted mural or wall painting. Other categories of wallpaper designs are printed in rolls from one long stencil, the entire length of the sheet. These are then rolled up in specific lengths and sold in rolls.

We will turn now to a brief glimpse of the make-readies used in commercial printing houses which do textile or wallpaper screening.

Commercial textile printing establishments operate as a big business in terms of equipment, floor space, steaming and other facilities. The typical large scale textile screening shop employs craftsmen whose training and experience are limited to that phase of screen process to the exclusion of general advertising printing techniques.

Here is the setup of a typical screen printing table for printing large yardages of goods. The table is from 60 to 80 yards long, 64 inches wide, and professionally constructed of wood or metal. A length of 60 yards is generally sufficient for the processing of all kinds of silk materials, whereas for processing cotton goods a length of 80 yards is necessary. A width of 64 inches is necessary for handling standard bolts of cloth. The wood type tables are covered with a layer of extra-heavy felt or foam rubber all in one piece without seams. On top of this soft padding is tightly stretched a covering of extra-heavy oilcloth or similar material. Fans are distributed overhead or at each side at regulated intervals to hasten the drying. Textile printing tables constructed of metal have the advantages of more rigid construction and built-in heating systems. The top is composed of asbestos plates, which retain the heat without expanding or warping the printing base.

The cloth is laid out on the table as it is pulled from a ratchet arrangement roller holder. The cloth is then stretched crosswise by fastening it to the table with pins or special easy-to-remove staples. All along the top of the table, extending its full length, is a metal rail to which are attached "contact stops" or register guides. These stops are placed at fixed intervals along the rail and fastened in place with thumbscrews. The distance between these register stops is adjusted to the size of the unit or design repeat. The stencil frame is made to fit the table. 1¼" screw eyes are placed near each end of one of the narrow sides of the frame to serve as sliding contacts for the rail (Figure 86).

The print is made in alternate register areas. The stencil is held by the short end and placed in position on the cloth by means of contact stops, and a print is pulled by drawing the squeegee toward and away from the operator, up and down. The screen is then lifted, a gap is left unprinted, and another print is made. Again, a gap is

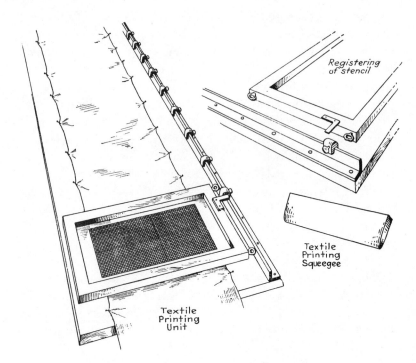

Registering
of stencil

Textile
Printing
Squeegee

Textile
Printing
Unit

FIG. 86. Textile screening table for hand screening of bolt material. This system employs register stops adjusted mathematically to the size of the pattern repeat.

left unprinted. When the entire length is complete, the alternate gaps are printed. If everything has been done correctly in the matter of registration, the all-over design on the cloth will appear continuous without evidence of breaks or unmatched connections. Since the heat makes the color dry faster, it is not necessary to wait with the filling-in of the alternate gaps until the end of the line has been reached. The gaps are filled by another operator who follows with another stencil, either applying the same color or the next color in a multicolor design. The job is not finished yet. After printing is completed in all colors, the cloth is untacked and put through a finishing process. Most colors require an additional steaming to set the color permanently. The cloth is then put through a continuous washer, traveling through several tubs, the first of which contains a soap solution, the other merely containing plain water for rinsing. The material passes through a "hot box" for drying, is again "framed" back to its original width, then run through a calendaring press for further softening and ironing, and finally bolted for shipment.

If "discharge" colors are used, the material goes through the same lengthy finishing operation described above, except that it is given a four-minute steaming to "develop" the color, before it goes to the 35-minute steam "fastening" process. Repitigen colors are developed by an acid fume system and are then given the same treatment as application colors. The acid fumes bring out the latent chroma of the colors. This description, which has turned out less brief than we had originally intended, does not even touch upon the involved chemistry of dye formulation which is guarded jealously by tight-lipped dye specialists.

It is interesting to note that no one commercially prepared textile color can be used for all textile printing jobs. One paint catalog frankly concludes with this self-protective caution to the user, "All textile colors are sold without warranties expressed or implied."

We have gotten so involved in the description of commercial textile printing that we will have little space left for a presentation of commercial wallpaper screening. In a sense, the procedure is similar except that it does not involve the washing and steaming. The tables are steam heated; the prints are made in alternate gaps, to be filled in as separate operation. Another method of wallpaper printing, quite different from this, is one employing a rotary machine for continuous roll printing.

There is an extensive market for piece goods printing. Quite apart from screening on dress goods material, which, as we have seen, requires extensive equipment, printing on piece goods in most cases is accomplished with existing poster printing equipment, altered in some instances with jigs and make-ready adjustments. There is a growing demand for such specialty work on T-shirts, pennants, souvenir pillow cases, advertising banners, tablecloths, draperies, novelty and advertising aprons and a host of miscellaneous fabric products. All of these and others, flat goods and fabri-

FIG. 87. Modern rotary belt screening table designed for towels and similar piece good material. As many as six colors can be set up in tandem so that the material is printed in all colors in one cycle. (*Courtesy Precision Screen Machines Co.*)

cated, are successfully screen printed today. While we have concentrated in this chapter on cloth and paper, we must not forget other flexible materials such as vinyls and an array of other plastics which go into the making of shower curtains, book covers, lamp shades, game cloths, charts and table mats. The list could almost be expanded indefinitely.

There are divisional specialties within the textile printing industry. In Patterson, Passaic, and other parts of New Jersey, where many of the silk screen textile printing firms are situated, there is, for instance, one company which has made a specialty of silk screening tablecloths and decorative hand towels and similar piece goods. The entire plant is set up for that type of operation. Using automatic textile screening presses, this firm operates on a steady production schedule of over one hundred dozen towels per hour for each unit. Each machine is more than one hundred feet long and has a hook up of four to six different color stencils, synchronized to print in sequence, each applying one color without any interlude of drying. The complete printing cycle is automatic. Feeding and take-off are manual. The operation consists of placing the unprinted towel on a moving rotary belt conveyer. The material clings to the waxed surface of the belt, is carried in its fixed position in register through the multicolor stencils, and drops off completely printed at the other end of the machine. The material is then hung over bamboo sticks which in turn travel up an escalator track into an overhead drying oven. The material continues to travel within the oven for a cycle of five minutes. The 350° F. heat of the oven absorbs the water content of the special emulsion paint and sets the color pigment permanently into the fibres of the cloth. The entire cycle from raw material to the finished and cured print is 15 minutes. Once the material leaves the oven it is ready to be packed. No further treatment or processing is necessary. The finished print is fast, completely washable and bleach-proof.

Figure 88 shows the interior of such an establishment with custom built textile printing presses engineered by the Precision Screen Machines Company of New Jersey.

Fig. 88. Interior view of an up-to-date textile printing plant, showing some of the modern press equipment in use. (*Courtesy Precision Screen Machines Co.*)

16. AUTOMATION

IT MAY seem odd that in an era of push-button mechanization, printing by screen process was done almost exclusively by hand until after the middle of this century. While the rotary presses of other graphic arts were whirling away at speeds of upwards of 10,000 impressions an hour, the screen printer drudgingly sweated out 250 or so impressions an hour with the aid of a helper. It was not for want of ingenuity in designing automatic presses that silk screen lagged doggedly behind its competitors. Power-driven screen presses had been in operation as far back as 1925 which were capable of speeds of 1200 impressions per hour. The drawback was mainly in the fact that the paints available at that time were not formulated to dry quickly enough to keep up with the fast pace of the press. It used to take hours, sometimes overnight, for some paints to dry. Each print had to be placed in a separate shelf in a rack for prolonged air drying. No shop could possibly have enough drying racks or the floor space to keep a 1200-impression-an-hour press in operation for an eight-hour day, so that there was no practical demand for a press.

The demand for faster drying paints was foreseen by paint chemists, who, working closely with press and drying engineers, evolved paints which were formulated to dry within minutes, and with which the time could be further reduced to seconds via forced drying ovens. The close cooperation, therefore, between the experts of the paint laboratories, press and drying engineers brought about the mechanization which had lagged for years.

As we have said elsewhere, it is unlikely that automatic presses will ever completely replace hand processing. However, the trend in mechanization is destined to continue, especially in those areas of screen printing where standardization is possible.

We have seen in the chapter on paint (Chapter 9) the array of color compounds chemically formulated for fast drying and designed to be used in conjunction with automatic printing and drying equipment. Let us now examine the developments that have taken place in the last few years in each of the two areas—drying equipment and automatic press printing.

DRYING EQUIPMENT

There are a number of systems for forced drying: circulating air drying, infra-red electric heat, gas heat, etc.

Air Drying

Among the outstanding equipment in this method of air drying is the type of "Wicket Dryer" shown in Figure 89. This is an endless belt on which are attached upright lightweight rack metal shelves which travel in a circuit. These wire trays or wickets hold the wet print in an inclined upright position and circulating air naturally dries the paint as it travels the length of the unit. One complete cycle on a 10-foot unit carries the drying stock for a distance of 20 feet. One 10-foot unit has the same capacity as 8 standard hand rack loads of 50 racks each, yet it occupies only ¼ of the space which would be required if stationary racks were used.

Wicket dryers are available in several sizes. A standard 10-foot chassis has a capacity of 375 trays. The size of the wicket ranges from 22″ x 45″ to 45″ x 65″. Special sizes can be had on a custom-built basis. The chief advantages of this air drying wicket rack system is that the print dries without heat and, therefore, without shrinkage or distortion. Also, the unit requires comparatively little floor space and can be had on a movable platform for greater flexibility. It is operated on a variable speed drive and can be set up in conjunction with an automatic take-off device which will take the ejected sheet from the press and set it on the wicket

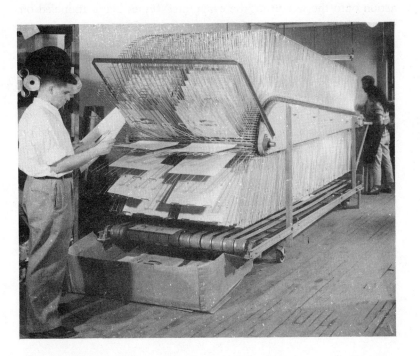

FIG. 89. Wicket drying rack, a space-saving system for air drying of prints. (*Courtesy American Screen Process Equipment Co.*)

for its cycle of drying. After the sheet has completed its drying cycle, it is deposited on a receiving stack, ready for the next operation. Operational speed is 1200 to 1500 sheets per hour.

Heat Drying Equipment

There are several sources of heat used for drying: gas heat, oil heat and electric infra-red heat. Gas and oil heat have proven themselves more adaptable to the needs of screen process than electric heat.

Gas and oil heat units. These units consist in the main of a canvas or metal conveyer belt which carries the wet print through a heating oven, then to a cooling unit. The gas heat generated in the oven is not "dead" heat; rather, it is forced with a jet pressure action onto the wet print, the evaporated fumes being funneled off into an opening vent leading to the street. Commercially known as "jet dryers," these units, of which there are several excellent ones on the market, operate on thermostatically controlled heat, regulated for rapid evaporation of ink solvents. Variable temperature settings assure different heat adjustments for different printing compounds and stocks. The unit consists of a conveyer, a heat oven and a cooling bin. In the complete cycle, the wet print is placed on the conveyer belt, travels through the heat oven, passes the cooling bin, and is carried to the drop-off terminal of the belt at the other end.

Actually the jet dryer is an indirect drying system. The open flames do not contact the circulating air during any portion of the complete drying cycle. Incoming air sweeps around the combustion chamber and the heated air sweeps down into the drying chamber and uniformly pressurizes the area. Pressure forces the turbulent hot air through a multitude of tiny holes in the grid base of the drying chamber. Hot air comes out as a forceful jet stream that is blown

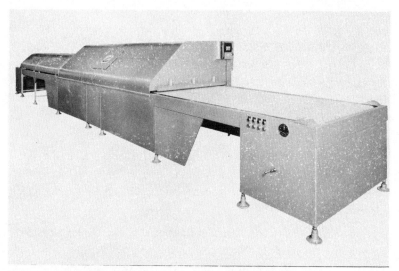

Fig. 90. The Cincinnati Jet Dryer, one of the popular drying units in use today. (*Courtesy Cincinnati Screen Process Supplies, Inc.*)

onto the passing wet print, with uniform pressure at all points.

With the use of jet dryers, the time required to dry many inks, paints, resists and other media is reduced to seconds through acceleration of evaporation. These units come in various sizes, width and length of conveyer, capacity of heating and cooling chambers and over-all floor space (Figure 90).

Electric infra-red dryers. Infra-red is a method of heating by radiation. The drying ovens using this heating system employ clear type infra-red lamps and gold-plated reflectors which distribute the heating action evenly throughout the surface of the print. Both the amount of heat and the distribution of it can be regulated by switch controls of different zones of lamps. There is also a cooling chamber which operates by means of fans. There are several models. One, with a one-minute drying cycle, will dry approximately 500 28″ x 44″ sheets per hour, or 1000 22″ x 28″ sheets. Infra-red electric ovens are somewhat more costly to operate and are best for lightweight work which does not require high temperature drying.

AUTOMATIC PRESSES

Tremendous progress has been made lately in the development of automatic screen printing presses. Presses are on the market to meet the needs of the varied requirements in terms of thickness and nature of stock, size of printing surface, available floor space, and degree of automation. Here are a few examples:

One line of presses engineered by the General Research and Supply Company comes equipped with an automatic feeder and take-off and is designed for printing 19″ x 24″ sheets at up to 3000 impressions per hour (Fig. 91). The presses in this category, however, are limited to thin flexible stock, up to 10 pt. board, although an optional delivery attachment is available for printing board up to 40 pt. The quality of printing is superior to manual printing, with accuracy of register under constant mechanical control. Standard wood frames can be used. Pressure is fully maintained over the entire length of the squeegee. Larger models, retaining these same features, are in stock.

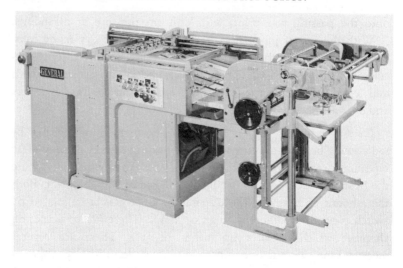

FIG. 91. The Model 24 General Press, capable of speeds up to 3000 impressions per hour. Maximum printing size, 19" x 24". (*Courtesy General Research, Inc.*)

Another line of General machines is the Decorator Presses. These are precision-built presses engineered for screen process printing of any rigid material, such as metal signs, heavy boards, wood, wall board, etc. The three basic elements are a reciprocating open bed on rails which supports and carries the material to be printed, a reciprocating stencil frame and a stationary squeegee under the moving stencil frame. The cycle is as follows: The material to be printed is front and side registered automatically and is picked up by the bed. During the printing stroke, vacuum holes in the printing bed hold the sheet firmly in position as the bed passes underneath the stencil and the squeegee. The press has a continuous cycle with a variable speed drive. The print travels in a straight line from feed-board through printing through delivery at the other end of the press. Speeds are up to 1800 impressions an hour. Although the standard models in this series are designed for thickness of stock no more than 3⁄4", presses can be ordered for extra-heavy stock up to 6" in thickness. The General Model 34, designed to print sheet sizes up to 24" x 34" at speeds up to 3500 per hour, is engineered for precision printing of small intricate

FIG. 92. The General Model 76 completely automatic press designed to screen sheet sizes up to 52″ x 76″ at a maximum pace of 1500 impressions per hour. (*Courtesy General Research, Inc.*)

work, such as greeting cards, decals, plastic sheet printing, foil printing, etc. Make-ready is moderately simple and registration accurate and automatic. It features a delivery system which holds each sheet in position as it travels.

The big General press unit is General's Model 76, equipped with automatic feeder and take-off (Figure 92). This is excellent for extremely large sheet sizes in posters, 24-sheet and folding cartons. It takes a 52″ x 76″ sheet at speeds of 1500 impressions per hour and is completely automatic.

Ink distribution is automatically controlled and, like all such presses, it can be run with split fountains. Some of the large General presses hooked up in tandem with jet dryer units make for an impressive combination of high speed production with quality control, but they are specifically designed for large runs.

Not all screen presses are as elaborate. Various other manufacturers (listed in the Sources of Supply chapter) feature presses for smaller dimensions in varying degrees of automation. The Lawson "Genie" series comes in models which are automatic only in the actual squeegee operation. Feeding is manual. The operator con-

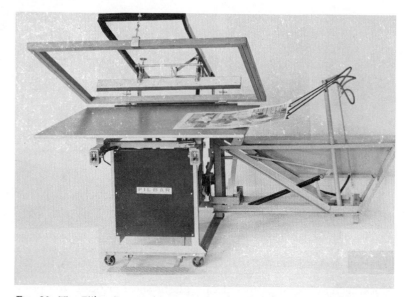

FIG. 93. The Filbar Press, with automatic take-off device. Its versatility permits it to print on both rigid and flexible material at speeds adjusted to the nature of the material. It is comparatively inexpensive but sturdy in construction. (*Courtesy Graphic Equipment of Boston, Inc.*)

trols the speed of the press to suit the needs of the material that he is printing. Models came in a wide range of printing sizes from 16″ x 22″ to 48″ x 72″ with a variable speed up to 1000 impressions an hour, and are good for any flat surface up to one-inch thick.

Fig. 93 shows a simple screen press with automatic take-off device. Only the feeding is manual. The operation of the squeegee and the ejection of the print are automatic. This press, marketed as the Filbar Press, has a variable speed drive up to 900 impressions per hour. It features a foot-operated brake to stop the press instantly during any part of the cycle. Its steel surface vacuum bed makes it ideal for printing on paper as well as for board of any thickness. The automatic take-off device, synchronized to the variable speed of the press, removes the printed material and sets it on

FIG. 94. The Precision Industrial Screen Printer, versatile but especially well suited for screening printed circuits and other industrial fabrications. (*Courtesy Precision Screen Machines Co.*)

a conveyer belt for drying. The Filbar Press is at present available in three standard sizes: 30″ x 45″, 35″ x 45″ and 44″ x 65″.

There are presses designed for specific industrial production where silk screen printing is a related phase of manufacturing. One such press, the Precision Industrial Screen Printer, shown in Figure 94, will print on any material with a flat top surface. The printing stock may be rigid, limp, square or irregular-shaped—anything from thin paper to material one inch or more in thickness. Though it is versatile in its use, this unit is exceptionally well suited for the production of printed electric circuits. Special tops can be interchanged to accept a variety of fixtures. The press features a "dwell-time" control which allows printing at maximum speeds at all times. Only the open time of the print cycle is regulated to whatever time is necessary to lead and take off the stock. The operator can register the difficult or easy type of work at whatever speed is most practical.

There is a market for presses which are engineered to be semi-automatic in the sense that feeding and take-off are manual. The operation of the squeegee is mechanized. Such presses often offer singular advantages over the completely mechanized units because they permit the operator to regulate his own pace. This is important when printing difficult-to-handle materials like glass, heavy masonite, or such flexible or odd-shaped stock as cloth, die cut displays, heavy panels, etc. These presses are in the main less expensive and more versatile. Being basically simple in construction, they can be built economically and in large as well as small sizes. One manufacturer offeres a 48″ x 112″ model, which he calls a Powered Squeegee. This semi-automatic unit can print on any material that the conventional hand-operated printing unit can handle. It can be used on paper, glass, masonite, wood, vinyl, etc. with simple adjustments in make-ready. Everything here is the same as for the conventional manual screen unit, except that the squeegee moves across automatically when the screen frame is lowered.

The average screen shop may not be geared for complete automation for several reasons. The type of work it does may be too varied for standardized equipment. Then, too, installation of heavy equipment often involves an expenditure beyond the means of the modestly financed processor. If this is the case, the semi-automatic equipment mentioned above may prove to be worth considering. Among other printing equipment even less expensive is a line of squeegee units variously called, "One-man squeegee," "Easy squeegee," etc. Several firms, principally the Kenn Equip-

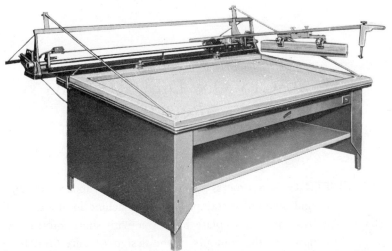

FIG. 95. The "One-man squeegee," an efficient manual printing unit with a patented counterbalanced squeegee device. (*Courtesy Cincinnati Screen Process Supplies, Inc.*)

ment Company and the Cincinnati Screen Process Supply Company, have done much to develop this type of operational equipment. In the main, these units consist of a heavy squeegee bar which rides smoothly along a back rail. The squeegee's counterbalance serves to apply pressure to the rear end. The operator exerts some pressure to the front end, but actually *guides* more than bears down on the squeegee. This type of squeegee arrangement is efficient for printing large areas which require a very big squeegee and normally a team of two men and considerable effort to get an even distribution of paint across the large printing surface. The principal advantage of this unit is that it cuts a two-man job down to a one-man operation. It is not only less physically fatiguing than the conventional squeegee pushing operation, but is considerably faster in production and much more uniform in quality (Figure 95).

Other semi-automatic and completely automatic presses for printing cylindrical surfaces, flocking and odd-shaped objects are discussed in Chapters 13 and 14.

17. FACTS ON DIE CUTTING AND FINISHING

DIE CUTTING is a process whereby paper, cardboard, or any flexible or rigid material is stamped out by machine in any desired shape. This is done with a plate fitted out with sharp protruding steel rules shaped to the contours of the design (Figure 96). It is the stamping process used in the production of window displays, floor stands, "pop out" cut-outs, and point-of-purchase merchandisers. It is the same means which is used commercially to stamp out cardboard jigsaw puzzles and other irregular-cut novelties in mass production. If one or two or even a dozen cut-out displays are required, they would not be die cut. The chances are they would be cut out either by hand with a mat knife, or by electric cut-awl machine or jig saw. It does not become practical to get a die made unless the quantity of cut-outs needed is more than can be economically produced by hand. A die is costly and involves some of the machine operations which we will discuss in this chapter.

Let us take a hypothetical design: a simple silhouette cut-out of the life size figure of a little girl, to be used as a store display attraction. The screen printing is done on the usual rectangular proportioned card, in this case, let us say, 36" x 60". In printing this job, the colors edging the shape to be die cut must be overdrawn, that is, made ¼" or so larger all around, to allow for the required margin for trim-off. This is known as a bleed. When the printing is complete, the screen printer must prepare an accurate mark-out sheet so that the die cutter will have an exact template to

176

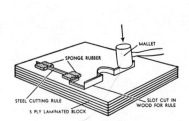

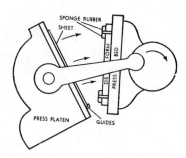

FIG. 96. A die cutting plate in preparation. The steel die, shaped to conform to the outline of the design, is hammered into the grooves of the wood plate.

FIG. 97. The action of the die cutting press makes the steel rule come into contact with the material to be cut.

follow. This master mark-out sheet is then sent to the die cutter to serve as a tracing pattern for his die.

When the die cutter gets the mark-out sheet, he makes a careful pencil tracing of the outline and retraces the form onto a ⅝″ plywood, large enough for the tracing. With a power jig saw, he cuts over the tracing, the saw blade making a 1/32″ track through the wood. Using a flexible steel rule strip, he hammers it into this track and bends the steel rule to conform to the curvature of the silhouette (Figure 96). The steel rule about 1″ high extends approximately ¼″ above the surface of the plywood plate. Then bits of sponge rubber pads are glued to the plate, adjacent to the steel rule, to serve as spring cushioners to push the cut material out. The plate is then adjusted to a press in many ways similar to a printing press, except that this press holds a steel die plate rather than a printing plate (Figure 97). The 36″ x 60″ card is then fed into register guides, or "grippers," as the die cutter calls them. The meeting of the die and the card, under pressure, sinks the steel rule die into the card and cuts it through, pretty much as a cookie cutter cuts soft dough. Very careful make-ready is necessary to regulate the depth of penetration of the blade to correspond to the thickness of the cardboard.

If the die does not penetrate deeply enough, the cut will be incomplete, if too deep, the steel rule blades will be impaired. But the particulars of make-ready in this area are within the province of the die cutter's art and need not concern us here. It is important, however, for the screen processor to know the general procedure of die cutting as it involves both his designing the art work and screening the job.

DESIGNING FOR DIE CUT DISPLAYS

An example of an impractical design would be the silhouette of a boy holding in his hand a long extended fishing rod. This might look clever on the original drawing as it reposes on the artist's drawing board, but it would not be a practical job for die cutting. Why? Simply, because the extended strip of cardboard of the fishing pole would be a vulnerable point in the operation of die cutting, handling, shipping and assembly. A thin strip of unsupported cardboard would easily break somewhere in the process and what appeared like a clever design in concept would turn out to be a poor production venture in practice. The artist can often simulate the desired effect by introducing a background element into his design which provides the necessary stability, yet carries the desired illusion. For instance, instead of that slim fishing pole extending in isolation well beyond the main body of the display, it could be structurally strengthened by the introduction of a background scene, a cloud or other design element appropriate artistically as well as practically.

Another caution to observe in creating a design which is intended for die cutting is to avoid a preoccupation with such detailed intricacies as fine cogs of a wheel, lacy frilly lattice work, etc. Theoretically, a die may be made for any design. But the cost factor in making a frilly die and the loving care required in handling the cut displays make such designs rather impractical commercially. It is a good policy to limit oneself to art simple in silhouette, devoid of fancy filigree. This does not mean that the designer creating a cut-out display is to be forced into routine pedestrian shapes of simple silhouettes. Ingenuity need not be stifled. Some very dramatic and novel displays may be planned for die cutting and produced effectively and economically.

SCORING AND FOLDING

By regulating his knife and make-ready, the die cutter can control the depth of knife penetration so that the card is not cut all the way through. This is known as a cut score and is important in display and box construction. Scores make possible sharp turns in the structural components of three-dimensional displays. Three-

FIG. 98. An interesting example of a three-dimensional window display designed for flat shipping and easy setup. (*Courtesy Interstate Boochever Co., Fairlawn, N. J.*)

wing self-supporting window displays, floor stands, counter displays, platform and step pedestals, are some typical examples. The die cutter can alter at will the type of rule he uses in his die. Thus, by substituting a dull or thicker gauged rule for the razor-sharp steel rule, the impact of rule and card will result in a deep but uncut impression, needed for creasing and folding structures. Planning of display material for cutting, scoring, easy assembly and compactness in shipping is an art in cardboard engineering which represents a career speciality to those gifted in visualization, mathematics, and fundamental three-dimensional structural design. Most large display design firms as well as die cutting firms and lithographers operate a bull pen to perform this creative branch of the merchandising business. This department often includes specialists in motor-driven motion displays, "spectaculars," mobiles, shadow box displays, and other ingenious, eye-catching, three-dimensional promotional novelties of motion, light and color.

MOUNTING AND LINING

Mounting generally refers to the machine-pasting of a sheet of paper (or other material) onto a cardboard. In the process, the paper receives an even coating of paste and the paper sheet and cardboard base are brought together under pressure. This is the process used to paste a "liner" paper such as litho, kromekote, or other good quality paper onto a cardboard of the desired thickness.

Lining on the other hand refers to pasting, too, but from a *continous roll,* rather than in *sheet* form. Each paper is not handled separately and mounted as a single sheet but rather run from one giant roll of the selected paper stock. Since it is a continuous roll feeding, lining is a considerably faster operation than mounting. It is good to remember that the mounter may line not only the conventional white and colored papers, but can also handle flint, glazes, metal foils, embossed papers, etc.

VARNISHING

Most die cutters do mounting and finishing as part of the

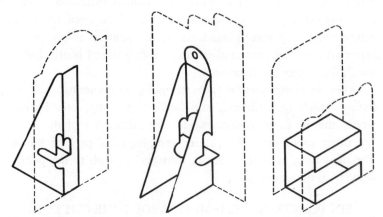

FIG. 99. Single-wing easel.   FIG. 100. Double-wing easel.   FIG. 101. Box easel.

general service they render. In addition they often equip themselves with facilities for "spot" and "all-over" varnish coating. Varnishing is used to create a gloss or a protective coating on printed sheets. It may be an all-over coating, which means that the entire area of the sheet is coated with varnish, or the area of varnish may be restricted to limited portion of the printed sheet, as in spot varnishing.

Although the operation is referred to as "varnishing," either varnish or lacquer may be used as the medium.

MISCELLANEOUS FINISHING OPERATIONS

In addition to die cutting, mounting, lining and varnishing, most of the large die cutting firms render a complete service of varied other finishing operations. One of these is easeling. Easels are the self-locking cardboard supports for holding a cardboard poster in an upright position. There are several types of easels: single-wing, double-wing and box easels.

A single-wing easel (Figure 99) is, as the name suggests, a single extension or wing which acts as a support and is usually attached to smaller posters. The double-wing (Figure 100) has a dual extension for more balanced support, and is reserved generally for large size posters. A box easel (Figure 101) is a rectangular collapsible support used to serve as a hidden extension platform for a projected plane in a display. Easels which need not be too substantial are generally made from inexpensive chipboard; the better type of easel material is jute, a tough fibred board, light in weight but rugged in structure.

Other finishing services are stringing, grommeting, and eye-letting, stitching, collating, slip-sheeting, packing, etc. In other words, the die cutter continues with the fabrication of the display (or other unit) after the printer completes his part of the job. The die cutter, in a literal sense, "finishes" the job to the point of delivery to the customer.

SIX POINTS TO REMEMBER ABOUT DIE CUTTING, MOUNTING AND LINING

1. When you order stock for a display which is planned for die cutting, consider the structure and grain of the finished display. Will the board be scored? Will it be folded? Is the stock heavy enough? Is the grain running in the right direction? Consult both with your cardboard supplier and die cutter for advice on the type of stock best suited to the needs of the job.

2. In designing art intended for die cutting, be practical in your structural design. Think not only of how beautiful the art work looks on the illustration board, but also how it will turn out in mass production. Think of the die cutter and do not add to his problems (and costs) by introducing impractical frills.

3. In making your stencils, always extend the paint at least ¼" beyond the cut outlines to allow for a trim-off for the die cutter.

4. Figure for a safe "over-run" to allow for spoilage for the die cutter. Just as inevitably as you spoil a certain percenage in printing, he will, too, in die cutting. If you give yourself a 5% spoilage, grant him at least half of that amount for his part of the work.

5. Give the die cutter an accurately traced mark-out sheet for his die. Indicate on it the sides and exact position of the register grippers. The printing and die cutting must be done from the same guide sides.

FIG. 102. A complete window display showing varied three-dimensional effects made possible by well-planned die cutting construction. (*Courtesy Poster Products Co., Chicago.*)

6. If a job is to be printed on a lined or mounted stock, do not print it immediately after the finisher delivers it to you, unless you know it is well seasoned. Freshly pasted stock must be "seasoned" to prevent warpage and shrinkage. Freshly mounted cardboard must be dried out either by racking, a trip through the oven or extended storage.

18. HOW TO PREPARE ART FOR SCREEN PROCESS

THERE IS an eternal conflict between the creative artist and the practical printer. It has been irreverently rumored that in the Hereafter, the artist will be made to do his own printing and the printer will be forced to design his own art. In that way, they can both be made to atone for their earthly indifference to each other's problems.

A good commercial artist who designs for printing should possess a good working knowledge of the technical limitations and latitudes of the particular process which will be used to reproduce his work. He should know beforehand the most suitable techniques which offer a minimum of technical or costly problems to the printer. The artist must always remember that it is not how "pretty" his original art work looks which matters. It is how well it reproduces which really counts—and which will ultimately reflect on his own professional reputation in the field. This does not mean that the printer should be freed of all technical problems just to make his job easy. The enterprising printer is himself creative and does not shy away from challenging problems. What the printer rightfully resents is the artist's supreme indifference to or ignorance of the technical and mechanical means of reproducing the art. It is therefore urged, for a better professional relationship between artist and printer, that they work together as closely as possible. In that way, the printer can carry out the artist's creative intentions, while the artist can be guided by the practical requirements of the printer.

184

The above practical philosophy applies to all graphic arts. Our present concern, however, is to offer suggestions for designing art specifically for the screen process. But since the scope of the process is so broad, it will serve our purpose best to relate the art requirements to specific stencil making methods.

The material discussed in this chapter will perhaps be more important to the freelance artist than to the artist who is employed as a resident staff member of a screen printing firm. The latter is thrown into daily contact with production and often works very closely with the stencil maker, paint mixer and other members of the printing department. Quite often, indeed, the stencil maker and artist are one and the same person, especially in the smaller shops. Such a person has the on-the-job experience to custom-make his design for the process. It is the self-employed free-lance artist or a member of an advertising agency art staff who only occasionally is called upon to design for silk screen who will benefit most by the guidance that is presented in the following pages.

ART FOR TUSCHE STENCILS

Art prepared for the tusche method allows for considerable latitude in textural and dry brush effects. In fact, an independent "fine art" offshoot of screen process is based almost entirely on the tusche method. This type of graphic art reproduction, called serigraphy, is a favorite among artists who generally like to do their own limited edition printing for exhibitions and galleries (Figure 103).

Art intended for commercial use is hardly ever designed for the tusche method because the results are somewhat uncertain, the line work is not nearly as sharp and the register of colors not as easily controlled. The artist working for industry, therefore, will do well not to design as freely as he likes on the easy assumption of "Oh, well, they can always print it with tusche stencils." If, however, after consultation with the printer, a commercial design is to be scheduled for the tusche method, the sketch should be in full color, same size, and confined to line, dry brush, solids and limited

FIG. 103. A serigraph print, *Flying Birdie*, by Leonard Pytlak, 1952. (*Courtesy National Serigraph Society, New York.*)

textural effects. It should be restricted to a limited number of colors. Although additional tones can be achieved in printing by using transparent colors, there are certain technical difficulties inherent in the nature of the job (but not obvious to the artist) which make this impractical. It is best, therefore, for the artist to proceed on the assumption that each color on his art work will require a separate stencil and a separate printing. However, for limited runs of pictorial designs, non-commercial in nature, the tusche technique offers interesting opportunities for experimentation and improvisation.

ART FOR THE PAPER STENCIL

The paper stencil technique (refer to Figure 42) lends itself to short runs, large lettering and simple shapes. The artist, in designing his art, should be guided by the fact that the stencil is cut out of paper. This means that the art easiest to reproduce is devoid of fussy lines and frills, or intricate configurations of shapes. Stipple, crosshatch, and similar textural art effects cannot be reproduced with paper stencils. Since the stencil cutter is concerned with outlines only, the lettering and other art elements on the sketch need not be filled in. The artist merely draws clean pencil outlines, indicating by notation the various color areas.

ART FOR THE HAND-CUT FILM STENCIL

The art work here may or may not be painted in color. If the design is simple and intended for printing in one or two separate colors, a pencil outline will do. The color areas can be indicated in one of two ways: one, by merely writing in the color, as a note to the stencil maker; two, by covering the design with a transparent tissue overlay and indicating the color areas in pastel or crayon. In either case, color swatches must be submitted for matching. The degree of finish or accuracy of rendering for this type of art is a matter of agreement and understanding between artist and stencil cutter. It is also a matter of mutal understanding between the designer and the client. Very often, although the actual technical requirement of screen process does not demand it, full-size finished colored art work must be submitted to the client who may not have the prior experience or the imagination to visualize finished results from a mere pencil outline sketch. He, like the gentleman from Missouri, must be shown to believe it—before he approves.

Again, it must be stated that for the freelance artist who does not work in close association with the stencil maker, it is best to assume that each color on the art work will require a separate stencil and a separate run. As a designer gains in his knowledge of the process, he will be able to take fuller advantages of technical possibilities to achieve the effects of additional colors without printing them.

If you plan art for hand-cut film stencils, keep the color areas moderately simple. Remember, even the simplest single line on your art work requires four distinct cuts before it can be stripped on film. The most acceptable art work for hand-cut film stencils is one which has a minimum of cross hatching, stippling, dry brush and other textural treatments. Several stencil methods may be combined on one design to achieve varied effects. Fine line work and small type matter too impractical to cut by hand may be reproduced by photo stencils. Dry brush and other textural effects are achievable by other stencil processes.

ART FOR PHOTO STENCIL TECHNIQUE

There is practically no limitation to art techniques for work intended for photo stencils. Straight line reproduction which includes lines, stipple, spatter, crosshatching and all textural effects —even printer's type as small as 6 pt.—all can be reproduced by silk screen photo stencils with excellent results. The thing to bear in mind is that the camera will pick up all that appears as black and white on the art work. This of course includes blemishes and other irregularities as well. The art for photo stencil reproduction may be larger, smaller or the same size as the intended reproduction. The photo positive can be reduced, enlarged or left the same size. Remember, the size may be altered, but not the proportions. Areas which are to appear as Ben Day (dots or patterns of even tone) may be introduced in the art by affixing commercial available Ben Day sheets, which when mounted in position on the art become an integral part of the design and appear as an additional uniform tonal effect. See the next chapter for fuller discussions of this.

Single Color Halftone Stencils

Theoretically, any sharp glossy black and white continuous tone picture photographically converted to halftone dots is acceptable for photo screen process. Theoretically, yes, but not without some technical qualifications. For general practical purposes, a 65-line halftone (equivalent to the size of the dots in the average newspaper photographs) is about the average dot size for large outdoor posters. Although there are examples of unusually fine silk screen prints produced with 133-line photo screens (the same fine quality used in glossy paper magazines), such silk screen prints are rare and therefore not as yet typical of the trade. For large sheet posters intended to be seen from moving vehicles on billboards, the 65-line halftone dots blend visually in the distance and are quite satisfactory. At close range, however, especially on such delicate subject matter as a baby's face or the close-up of a pretty girl, the dots may seem coarse and a finer dot must be used. The artist must exercise good judgment in creating a layout for halftone screen process reproduction. In the event that the selection seems to favor halftone work, all the artist needs to do in preparing his layout is to mount a contrasting, sharp photograph in position on the layout. From that, the stencil technician will order a "velox" print in a suitable halftone dot. The velox is a dot image transparency of the original photograph which changes a continuous tone into dots. The velox transparency becomes the photographic positive needed for photo screen making.

Art for Full Color Photo Technique

At the present writing, we cannot as yet encourage the artist to relax all practical restrictions as to technique, number of colors, experimental effects, etc. in the sanguine hope that his art work will be acceptable for the photo screen reproduction. Theoretically, the four-color halftone process, the basis of unlimited full color reproduction of lithography and letterpress, applies to screen process as well. In working practice, however, that is not the case, notwithstanding encouraging experimentation in that direction by several Western screen shops which have successfully reproduced water color paintings and oils, in unlimited natural colors. There are purists among the notable practitioners in the screen process field who think it is to the best interest of the craft to frankly stay within the technical poster technique limitations of the process. They deny the need of screen processors to imitate painfully (and often disappointingly) the results which are inherently within easy attainment of other graphic arts. There are others, equally honest workers in the field, who accept the apparent technical limitations merely as present challenges to be met and overcome in the future through continued experimentation and research.

THINGS TO REMEMBER IN DESIGNING
ART FOR SIILK SCREEN

1. Before proceeding with the design, discuss with the printer the particular art technique best suitable for the job. If possible, get actual samples of similar jobs previously produced. Seeing the original art work along with the reproduction is always helpful.

2. Unless impractical, render the art work the exact size of the intended reproduction, especially in multicolor work. This is especially important in a complicated piece of art work, which, when reduced or enlarged in black and white, loses much of the distinction in color values which distinguish one color from another.

3. The most acceptable (and often the best) art is that which is designed in a limited number of colors. Remember that in many cases each color you add means that you also add to the cost of production.

4. Keep color areas cleanly defined. Do not let colors carelessly blend or run into each other. This clarity of color definition is especially important where hand-cut stencils are to be used. Remember that the stencil man must cut all colors separately and in register with each other. He must know where one color area ends and another begins.

FIG. 104. A silk screened poster which in its simplicity and directness represents not only good art, but suitability for the process used to reproduce it. (*Courtesy McCann Erickson, New York.*)

5. Avoid subtle blends and air brush techniques, no matter how beautiful they look on the art work. They are often troublesome and impractical for silk screen.

6. If you are told that the job is scheduled to be reproduced in a given number of colors, confine yourself to the quota. Do not cheat and introduce additional colors or tones unobtrusively. They will find that out when they come to separate the colors in making the stencils, and either arbitrarily eliminate them, substitute existing colors—or substitute another artist for the next job.

There are a number of mechanical and photographic developments in the field which are of vital importance to the artist designing not only for screen process, but for any related graphic art. These developments are: (1) the Weber process, (2) the Bourges process, (3) photo-lettering, (4) shading sheets, (5) the hot press process. These will be discussed in the next chapter.

19. MECHANICAL AIDS FOR ART PREPARATION

IN THE last decade, many photographic and mechanical processes have been developed to aid the artist in the preparation of art work and copy for reproduction. This trend has not lessened his opportunities for creativity and originality. On the contrary, it has helped the artist to achieve his creative goals less laboriously and with greater latitude. A descriptive review of such methods, products and services is the business of this chapter.

BOURGES COLOR OVERLAY PROCESS

The Bourges sheets are patented color overlays which have had an almost revolutionary effect on the preparation of art for the printer. Widely advertised as the "Magic color sheet of 100 uses," the Bourges method (and similar systems) are widely used for layouts, package design, separation art, presentations, for color planning and special color effects. The Bourges method or system consists of a wide color assortment of transparent color acetate sheets with a special patented coating which can be easily scraped or washed away. There is a very wide assortment of colors, each available in different values and degrees of density. In essence, here is how the system works. The artist prepares his black and white art work in the usual manner. He then fastens a transparent sheet of the desired color over his black and white art. He scrapes or washes away certain areas of the sheet, leaving only those areas which are to appear in the color. What is the advantage of this method over the conventional way of applying color with brush and paint? Obviously, there are many advantages. Here are some. Since there is a wide assortment of Bourges color sheets available, the artist can try one color as easily as another. The color he chooses need not necessarily be the color he will finally use on the art work when it goes before the camera. In fact, often the artist is not sure beforehand which color will "go" best until he actually sees it combined with his key drawing. By using the Bourges transparent color sheets, he is free to experiment and to preview the effect without actually painting over his art. Once paint is applied over his art, it is obviously impossible to remove it, to try another color. With this process, therefore, it is feasible to experiment with colors easily without redoing the art work. What is more, the nature of the coating is such that the color is even, smooth and uniform in intensity and tone. There are no streaks or uneven brush blemishes. The artist and the customer are able to get a preview of the finished job as it will look in one color or any number of alternates. Moreover, because of the transparency of the sheets, several films of different colors may be superimposed in register over the art work thus combining the multiple color effects which are achievable with printing in transparent inks.

For the silk screen printer, the Bourges method offers the advantages of permitting him to prepare "hand-painted" color separations for photo stencils without the time-consuming effort entailed in the conventional method of applying opaquing ink with brush or pen. It is easier, faster, and more accurate to scrape away the coating on a Bourges sheet than it is to brush-paint on acetate. For large areas, a special "wash off" chemical is available which speedily removes the unwanted coating. Textural effects, line and large areas are all easily achievable. Not only do the Bourges sheets allow the artist to visualize the final color effect, but the color sheet itself becomes the color separation plate. The 100%, 70%, and 50% values of available color intensity of all Bourges color sheets are deep enough to provide the required contrast and permit the artist to work in true colors— blue, yellow, red, etc.—for camera copy.

The sheets come in pressure-sensitive adhesive films which can

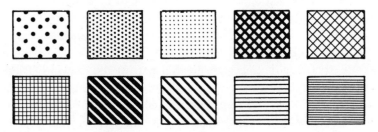

FIG. 105. A sampling of shading sheets which give the artist the widest latitude in tonal range and textural effects. (*Courtesy Cello-Tak Co.*)

be affixed directly over the art or in loose overlay sheets which are taped over the art, in register.

In a way, the Bourges sheet "color separation" method serves a purpose similar to that of the hand-cut ruby films developed by the Ulano Company. The Ulano ruby film is lacquer coated and the areas are removed by cutting with a stencil knife. However, for textural effects, dry brush and wash effects, the Bourges film has the advantage over the Ulano product.

It is advisable to have a working knowledge of all systems and methods to see where each best fits the needs of the job.

For particulars as to prices, sizes and range of colors, write to the Bourges firm, the address of which is listed in the chapter on "Sources of Supply."

SHADING SHEETS AND THE CRAFTINT PROCESS

Art work designed for photographic screen process reproduction may be planned to achieve the effect of additional tones of the same color with patented shading sheets. The use of shading sheets replaces the laborious and sometimes impossible job of crosshatching, dotting, stippling, or other tonal or textural effects which ordinarily might have to be attempted by hand. Thus, a one-color printing job may take on the appearance of several additional tones without additional printing costs or laborious art work.

These shading sheets are clear, transparent, self-adhesive films with an all-over design of dots (simulating Ben Day effects), crosshatch lines, spatter work, and hundreds of other different textural tones, each classified by number and density of pattern (see Figure 105). The artist merely selects the sheet with the texture that he needs, places it over his black and white art work, and scrapes off or cuts away the pattern where he does not want it. The pattern texture, therefore, becomes an integral part of the drawing. There are well over 200 catalogued sheets to choose from, in different densities as well as different textures and effects. A complete pattern sample book is available on request from either your process or your art dealer.

Shading effects are easily achievable by using still another method. This is a special illustration board patented by the Craftint Company. Here the artist prepares his black and white art in the usual way. But this board is different from the conventional type of illustration board. Chemically imprinted and invisible to the naked eye is a latent pattern which appears only when a companion chemical solution is applied. As if by magic, all areas touched with this colorless solution take on a pattern composed of dots, parallel lines, crosshatch, or other predetermined effect, selected from a catalog of patterns. These tones come out clear, black, and uniform in texture and are ideal for reproduction.

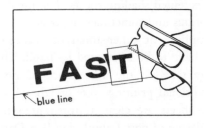

FIG. 106. Method of applying self-adhering lettering. (*Courtesy Cello-Tak Co.*)

PHOTO-LETTERING

A revolutionary change in the preparation of finished lettering has taken place in the last decade. The demand for the consummate skill of the reproduction lettering artist is declining constantly with the development of mechanical and photographic reproduction lettering devices. The art of the reproduction letter is being replaced by patented lettering sheets, photo-lettering and photo-lettering sources.

Lettering Sheets

These are transparent self-adhering acetate sheets with individual letters of the alphabet in a multitude of different standard type faces and sizes (Figure 106). There are several types. In one type, the characters are printed on the underside of the sheet and are simply transferred by rubbing to any smooth surface, assuring a sharp, clean-cut reproduction (Figure 107). Another type features an adhesive back. The adhesive back is not tacky, so that experimental positioning is possible. These sheets are available in a 10" x 14" size and are filled with complete alphabets, numerals, and punctuation marks in the same style. Letters are repeated on each sheet in the relative frequency in which they occur in the English language.

There are several other type-setting systems sold under various trade names such as Cello-Tak, Artype, Transfertype, Prestype, etc.

The Cello-Tak Company, one of the leading producers of trans-

Fig. 107. Method of applying transfer type lettering. (*Courtesy Prestype Co., New York.*)

fer lettering and shading sheets, publicizes the following features in its promotional advertisement:

1. The alphabets are printed on micro-thin transparent acetate. This assures easy assembly of the characters and perfection in reproduction. The paste-up marks do not photograph, thus touch-up is unnecessary.

2. Adhesive back. You can shift the letters all you want. They will not stick until you rub them with your fingernail.

3. Critically sharp. The lettering is as sharp as the best typographic proof.

4. Opaque black. No imperfections or pinholes in the print.

In addition to black opaque lettering, color type is available which can be applied by either the direct or transfer method. Similar features characterize the Prestype lettering sheets. Type face selection is very extensive, with point sizes going up to 120 point for some type faces. Alphabets are available in black as well as red, opaque white, blue and gold.

Photo-type Setting Machines

The Filmotype is one of a number of photo-lettering machines which enable the artist to set his own type photographically in his own studio. This unit is no bigger than a home tape recorder and is serviced with hundreds of type faces in various sizes. In addition to traditional type faces, there is at the artist's disposal a growing library of the finest in hand-lettered styles. This Filmotype unit (Figure 108) sets words or complete lines of copy with controlled spacing in the form of sharp black lettering on glossy paper strips. It is also possible to get tapes of clear acetate on which the lettering appears as sharp black opaque copy. No extensive photographic or typesetting skill is needed to operate this do-it-yourself photo-typesetting unit.

Another such unit, advertised as the Protype system, produces photocopy not in narrow strips requiring piece-meal paste-up, but in one-piece sheet areas as wide as 17". Point size is from six to ninety point.

The Varytype Headliner is still another photo-lettering unit.

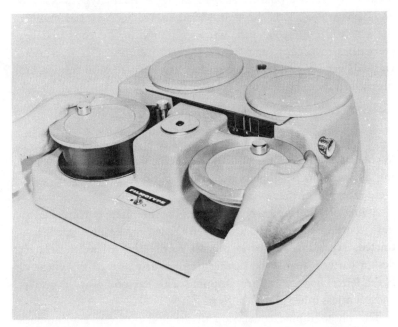

FIG. 108. The Filmotype machine, the studio do-it-yourself typesetter. (*Courtesy Filmotype Corp.*)

Here the copy is dialed on a rotating disk. In about 90 seconds a smudge-proof microsharp strip emerges ready for use. Type fonts are changed like phonograph disks and never wear out. The unit is simple to operate and requires no photographic experience. All developing, washing and fixing are automatic and self-contained. New photo-lettering systems are being developed constantly.

Photo-lettering Services

Today the talents of the finest reproduction letterers of the country are at your disposal via the photo-lettering service houses which serve the advertising and graphic arts industry. Specialty trade houses have sprung up all over the country whose sole business is providing photographically set lettering to the trade. Charges are very nominal and service by mail or pick-up is rapid. The large photo-lettering firms publish catalogs which list hundreds of original alphabets as well as the standard type faces. All you have to do is look through the catalog, select by serial number the size and style you need, write or phone in the copy and the space it is to occupy, and within a matter of hours or overnight, you will get beautifully set copy on glossy paper or on transparent film, all ready to be mounted on the layout.

THE WEBER PROCESS

This process, which bears the name of its exponent, Martin J. Weber, is an almost magical photographic system whereby lettering and art can be photographically altered in a variety of ways. Here are some of them.

A line of lettering or type can be photographically converted to italic, outline style or shadow lettering; it may be elongated, contracted, expanded, curved to any shape or repeated as an all-over design pattern. It may be further dramatically altered to appear as if the lettering were on fire, dripping with ice, going up in smoke, and countless other graphic effects.

The photographic conversion of art and illustrative techniques is equally prodigious. A water color painting, for instance, may be photographically rendered in the technique of a line drawing, stipple painting, or wood cut. It may be converted into distinct flat poster tones of any predetermined number. An ordinary photograph of an object, scene, or portrait may be photographically rendered in a variety of art techniques by employing the system of trick photography developed by the Weber Process.

This development has had a profound effect on the graphic arts and an equal impact in the field of commercial art preparation. It has freed the artist from many of the tedious, though skill-requiring tasks of his trade. It has helped to shift the artist's attention to more original concepts in the creative realm of layout and design. Not only has the Weber system reduced costs and cut time of production of art, it has also raised the standards of craftsmanship and fidelity of representation beyond human bounds. For instance, with this system a photographic close-up of a complicated cross section of a jet motor or other machine can be converted into a pure line drawing (or any other art technique) with an exactitude impossible to duplicate by hand. The Weber process is now widely used for preparing art for silk screen and other printing methods, newspaper and magazine work, and for practically every branch of the advertising field. This process cannot be installed or practiced by the individual user. It is not a "process" in the sense that you buy something tangible. It is really a professional service to the trade, operating on the same basis as the photo-lettering services previously mentioned.

HOT PRESS PROCESS

The photo-lettering systems mentioned above are limited to black and white reproduction and a few select colors. With the Hot Press process, the artist has at his disposal sharp reproduction proofs in full color (including gold and silver leaf) which can be applied directly to any flat surface. Indeed, the earlier use made of this process was for stamping gold and silver leaf inscriptions on leather and cloth book bindings, initials on luggage, etc.

In essence, this is how the process works. The card (or other material) which is to receive the lettering is registered on a metal plate. Standard printer's type is set up and locked in a chase in an overhead position. A sheet of colored leaf from a spool at one end is rolled over to cover the type. Electrically operated with a high degree of heat and pressure, the type is made to bear down on the printing surface. The force of heat and pressure imbeds the colored leaf into the surface, the impression corresponding to the type setup.

Advantages of the Hot Press process are:

1. Colors are bright and opaque.

2. It can be used on many surfaces—thick or thin, opaque or transparent. It is as good on illustration board as it is on transparent acetate or any other material.

3. An extensive range of type faces is available, both as to style and size.

4. Hot Press transparencies can be used as color overlays on original art work or as positives for photo screen process.

5. Once the setup is made, it costs very little more to get multiple copies.

6. The service is fast and the range of prices nominal.

It is urgently recommended to the artist designing for screen process (or indeed for any other graphic art) that he acquaint himself fully with the modern aids described in this chapter and that he extend his knowledge of them through individual inquiry and experimentation.

20. SILK SCREEN AS A
FINE ART MEDIUM

IT TOOK the depression years of the early thirties to introduce the silk screen process to the art world. During that dark period in our economic life, the Government had set up many "make-work" emergency agencies designed to keep men productively busy and off the streets. One of these agencies was the Graphic Arts Unit, which provided experimental art facilities and a minimal pay check to needy artists. The Unit comprised easel painters, print makers, and the unemployed among the commercial artists, letterers and graphic designers. It was one of the tasks of this group to design and print posters and visual aids for various government agencies. It was found that the most expedient way to reproduce these posters in full colors was by the silk screen process. The process was comparatively simple and inexpensive, and it called upon the varied talents and skills of designers, letterers, illustrators and paint mixers. It was also found that the process permitted many personal improvisations and explorations which extended beyond the limited range of conventional techniques in poster making. This attracted artists and fine print makers. A special group was set up for using the process experimentally as a fine art medium— and the results were very interesting, not only in terms of technique —but in choice of subject matter as well. Favorite picture themes were the events and emotions of the depression itself—strikes, unemployment, hunger, interracial brotherhood, hope, despair and other graphic manifestations of social-conscious ideology.

The printed results were colorful as the artists who created them

Fig. 109. Serigraph, *Circus, 1958*, by Eugene Chodorow, 1958. (*Courtesy National Serigraph Society, New York.*)

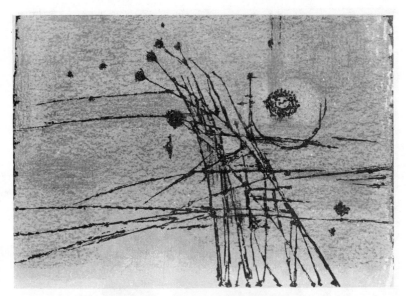

FIG. 110. Serigraph, *Morning Lines,* by Edward Landon, 1957. (*Courtesy National Serigraph Society, New York.*)

—many of whom were well known in the field of the fine arts. Soon critics began to take favorable notice of this process, and this was followed by invitations to show silk screen prints in museums and galleries throughout the country. Long after the government art unit disbanded, the work of these artists continued to issue from their attic and home studios. The process gained distinction through the sensitive and colorful prints of a host of fine artists, such as Tony Velonis, Harry Sternberg, Elizabeth Olds, Harry Schokler, Adolph Dehn and many others.

Throughout the years since, the screen process as practiced by fine artists and print makers has continued to enlist the creative interest of artists and print makers throughout the world. In order to distinguish this phase of non-commercial print making from the purely industrial process, fine art screen printing is identified as serigraphy. The word is derived from *seri-,* meaning silk, and *graph,* which stands for print.

FIG. 111. Serigraph, *Forest,* by Louis Bunce, 1956. *(Courtesy National Serigraph Society, New York.)*

Although all of the stencil making techniques offer interesting opportunities for the serigrapher, the most popular method appears to be the tusche stencil technique. This may be because this method, more than others, is singularly responsive to individual treatment and improvisations. Tusche may be used in crayon or liquid form and allows for a wide range of textural as well as spontaneous brush effects. By placing an abrasive textured material such as sandpaper, canvas, leather, chicken wire, etc. directly under the silk and pressing over it with tusche crayon, a variety of both anticipated and accidental tonal effects comes to life. Liquid tusche allows for spatter, stipple, dry brush and other techniques of a spontaneous and personal character, not as achievable with any other stencil method (Figure 112). Tusche in crayon form is used for pastel texture treatments.

Color especially played an important part in the wide acceptance of serigraphy. Other fine art printing media can produce color prints, but none as readily and so prodigiously as serigraphy. It is as easy with the process to use the brightest circus red as it is to select the muffled, subdued tones of the pastel shades. In addition to the range of techniques and the almost unlimited color palette, the artist has equal latitude in the printing compound he may choose. He has at his disposal opaque oil base paints, transparent inks, temperas, lacquers, enamels, even adhesives for appliqués. This printing range is unparalleled in any other fine art printing medium. The colors can be laid on as thin and transparent as fluid ink or as opaque and impasto as gouache. The colors can be dull, semi-glossy or sparklingly shiny. And the printing may be done on paper, cardboard, canvas, plastic, fabric or any other flat surface whatever.

As unique and as diversified as these features are, the process might not have been quite as readily adopted if it entailed an expensive press or costly tools. With hardly more than a single portable screen and a squeegee, the print maker has at his disposal the wherewithal to create and produce hundreds (or thousands) of prints at a minimum material cost. He can construct his own stencil printing outfit and do the printing himself. He will need a squee-

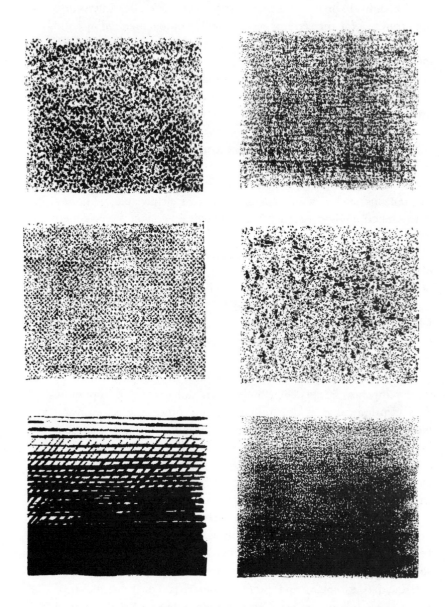

FIG. 112. A sampling of textural effects achieved with tusche.

gee, an investment which is small and permanent, and some paint and he is ready for his first creative efforts. The artist-print maker confining his output to a limited edition is not concerned with racks, drying ovens or the other heavy commercial equipment mentioned in this book. He will use a lot of paint only if he will do a lot of printing. If his initial experience with tusche leads to experimentation with the other stencil making methods, these, too, require but the simplest materials. Even if he were to use the photographic method (which is unlikely at first), the nature of his non-commercial work will call for hardly more than a piece of plate glass and a Fotoflood bulb or two. He will need kerosene or other reducers, but then he would require as much if he were to print from a woodblock or a lithographic stone. The cost of printing a serigraph will not exceed that of any other print form. The stencils will last for hundreds (or thousands) of impressions, and may be dissolved to allow for a new design using the same screen.

21. PLANT LAYOUT AND SHOP MANAGEMENT

IN ITS most elementary phase, screen process can be a "one- or two-man" organization. Fundamental equipment is comparatively simple and inexpensive. A dingy loft or ground floor store with a month's rent paid in advance may become the monumental theatre of operation. Indeed, many of our large shop owners of today look back with nostalgia and not without a feeling of pride at such humble beginnings. Years ago, an artist and his friend could get together as a team with a pooled investment hoarded from modest salaries earned on their respective jobs, to start out on this joint venture—the artist usually acting as creative and technical "inside" man, the friend (a good "dresser" and an aggressive extrovert) acting in the capacity of "outside" man or salesman. While the situation has changed somewhat today, owing to more aggressive competition and the trend toward expensive mechanization, it is still possible to get started in this modest fashion.

This chapter on plant layout will not, however, concern itself with this type of shoestring business organization. It would be too unreal to talk about a shipping department, offices, showroom, printing department or paint department if they were all one and the same thing, all occupying floor space the size of a large living room. We will, therefore, bypass this two-man organization with a nod of approval and gentle encouragement and turn our attention to a hypothetical screen process plant which is well equipped, well financed and departmentalized.

The ideal structure to house a screen shop is a steel and concrete building, with a sprinkler system, adequate passenger and freight elevators and loading platform facilities. It should have a smooth concrete floor and good ventilation. Plenty of window space and north light are very desirable. The best artificial illumination consists of long continuous fluorescent tubing well distributed throughout the shop, without dark spots or shadows. There is some sort of relationship, partly psychological, partly scientific, between the kind of illumination and shop morale, efficiency and craftsmanship. Poor, dim lighting casts a gloom on shop morale and tends to lower not only productivity but quality of work as well. Good lighting promotes higher standards of craftsmanship.

Location-wise, the shop should be situated away from congested truck traffic, yet sufficiently close to subways, buses and shipping terminals. Some of our metropolitan shops are moving into suburban areas, ofttimes unfortunately to the disadvantage of city resident employees, simply because truck traffic congestion causes expensive delays in delivery of stock and supplies and seriously retards schedules in the delivery of finished prints. Truck drivers have to waste considerable time waiting for clearance through dense traffic to pick up and deliver. Suburban screen shops often operate as tenant owner-operators of modern buildings specifically blueprinted to the needs of screen printing. These are generally one-level structures where all activities are carried out on one floor, thus eliminating the need for elevators and providing ample land for truck and passenger car parking.

FLOOR LAYOUT

It may be best at this point to take each "department" separately in reviewing its nature, needs and facilities. A model floor plan is shown in Figure 113.

Printing Department

This is the hub around which all departments rotate. It is the "shop" or factory wherein the actual printing is done. This requires the major floor area. The plan for the shop must make provision for manual as well as mechanized printing units, drying racks and

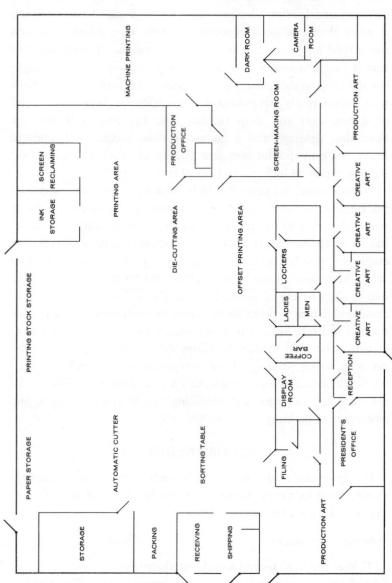

Fig. 113. Floor plan of a well laid out screen printing plant.

drying systems, and plenty of free aisle space for movement of stock and materials. A plant of about 20,000 square feet of shop space might include among its facilities three or four 50-foot conveyer drying ovens, several automatic presses of varying sizes, a half dozen or so manually operated screen tables, two dozen or so mobile drying racks, a power cutter for cardboard and paper, etc. Space must be allowed for storage of stocks and an active paper inventory. Provisions must also be made for storing hundreds of screen frames, extra printing bases, an assortment of squeegees of graduated sizes, as well as for facilities for easeling, flocking, tinseling, etc.

Since the rental costs in metropolitan areas are at a premium, ingenuity must dictate the best use of available floor space. Racks for screen storage can be off the floor, suspended on cantilever type structures; so can other light equipment and materials be stored on balconies without obstructing floor traffic or production.

Paint Department

Fire regulations in most cities prescribe specific storage facilities for housing inflammable printing compounds and solvents. A fire permit is granted upon the stipulation of a maximum quota of such material, based on approved facilities for storage. In most larger establishments, a well ventilated, well illuminated, fireproof room and sprinkler is structurally built in for this purpose. Within it, metal shelves of varying size and depth make for organized storage and easy access to a systematic assortment of different "lines" of color. For actual matching of colors, test screens are set up, usually near normal window light to obviate the need for matching color under any kind of artificial illumination whatever. Where normal light is impractical, or for work after sundown, a "daylight" blue type of fluorescent source of light is an acceptable substitute. The well equipped paint department will, in addition, have one or more electric paint mixers to expedite the rapid and complete mixture of printing compounds in large quantities. The department will also have an up-to-date, well tabulated file of color samples, a current

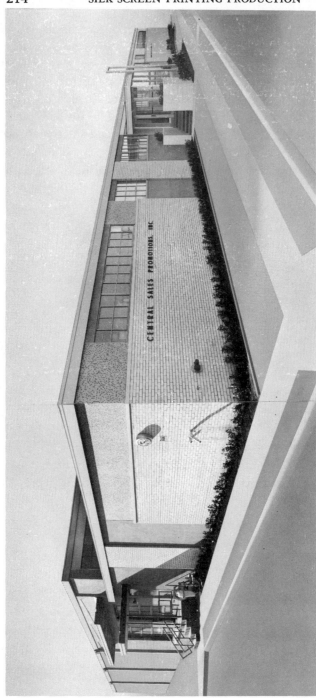

FIG. 114. An efficient screen printing plant is built from the ground up. This is the building which houses the modern plant and facilities of the Central Sales Promotions Corp. in Oklahoma City. The next seven illustrations are photographic views of the plant.

inventory record of standard and mixed printing compounds, as well as catalogs and color charts of suppliers.

Preparation Room

It is the job of this department to plan and build special jigs, construct screen frames, prepare and sharpen squeegees and have the necessary mechanical facilities for maintenance and shop repairs. It should also have facilities for manual or mechanical fabric stretching of screens. The setup may include a jig saw, rotary saw, electric planer and sander, drill press and other metal and wood fabricating equipment.

Stencil Making Department

This should include art tables, racks for temporary storage of screens, shelving and compartments for storage of supplies needed for hand-cut film stencils, tusche, paper and block-out stencils. This area should be equipped with a paper cutter for paper, card and

FIG. 115. Functional office and reception room.

other materials. Large map files should be available for storing cut stencil film, art work, photographic transparencies, etc.

Often this department is run in tandem with the art department. In that case, the combined department will include artists' drawing tables, a light table for touching up transparencies, a completely equipped artist's paint tabouret: brushes, rubber cement dispensers, tape dispensers, sample file, utility knives, cutting board for preparing mats and cut-out displays (by hand or cut-awl machine), photo-lettering units, etc.

Photo Stencil Department

Though many of our modern photo stencil films do not require darkrooms, it would be well to provide a constructed workroom for the preparation of all details involved in preparing photo stencils. This would include professional photographer's stainless steel sinks, with hot and cold water mixer, temperature regulator, vacuum exposure table and printer, etc. A well organized darkroom will have storage facilities for chemicals, presensitized film and all other paraphernalia—everything in its own place and readily accessible. The well equipped photo department will also have camera equipment for the making of transparencies, enlargements, reductions and photostats.

Shipping Department

This department, set up either as a special room or merely an allocation of floor space, should be logically situated near the freight elevator or loading platform. This would be equipped with scales for material weighing, lumber for construction of shipping crates, metal band strapping on a dispenser, an assortment of wrapping paper, cord, twine, shipping envelopes, etc. Many of the larger shops also have, in addition to several manually operated lift trucks, some of the heavier battery or electrically operated lift trucks and cranes to expedite stock handling. These power lift trucks, though costly, are tremendously efficient "work horses" for movement of stock, loading and unloading.

FIG. 116. Facilities for holding shirt-sleeve sessions where production problems are discussed and men are briefed to act as a coordinated team.

Finishing Department

The extent and nature of equipment for this phase of production will vary with each shop. There are some large screen printing organizations whose "finishing departments" include complete die cutting facilities, a business in itself. Others do their own assembly work on displays, easeling, mounting, pasting, flocking, etc. In its broadest sense, "finishing" implies all processes and operations which carry the printed displays one or more steps further in relation to the finished product. It is odd, but a fact nonetheless, that most of the larger establishments in the graphic arts industry— screen process, lithography, gravure, etc—do not handle their own complete finishing operations. This is the job for the finishers, mounters and die cutters who work with the printers on a pay-as-you-go competitive bid basis. However, many screen printing shops

FIG. 117. Creative art and stencil cutting department.

do their own easeling, flocking and other related operations, short of die cutting itself.

Office and Administrative Department

Office layout, décor, and equipment in a measure reflect the personality of the boss of the business. A disorganized, ill-equipped office, badly in need of a paint job, represents not so much an item of dollars-and-cents economy, as an index of instability in the physical or emotional makeup of the "boss." That bland statement naturally does not always apply to the facts on hand, but is true often enough to be passed off as an excusable generality on the part of a reflective observer.

In addition to standard office equipment consisting of desks, typewriters, adding machines, easy chairs, switchboard, files, etc., an office copying machine will serve a very useful purpose in the preparation of facsimile copies of correspondence, sketches, estimate

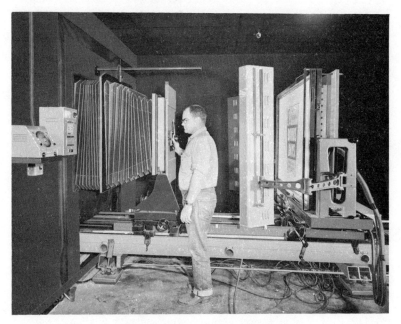

FIG. 118. View of camera room.

sheets and all other matter requiring multiple records. The office is frequently combined with a showroom where samples of screen work produced by the company are displayed with pride. Most of the larger shops also make provisions for a well-appointed conference room.

Wardrobe and Washroom Facilities

Adequate facilities must be set aside for the comfort and relaxation of employees: a place for proper wardrobe facilities, an area for eating lunch away from the interior of the shop, and a place to relax during free time. Washroom and toilet facilities should reflect a sense of concern for privacy and the physical hygiene of the workers in the "shop" as well as for the white collar employees in the front office and the administrative staff.

Figures 113–121 show the floor plan and a sampling of some of

FIG. 119. View of printing department, showing automatic printing and drying equipment in use.

the departments of the Central Sales Promotions Corporation of Oklahoma City, Oklahoma.

SHOP MANAGEMENT

Inasmuch as commercial screen process shops often operate on a close competitive basis, the shop manager, in order to meet or beat competition, must pay close attention to all production details. The elimination of minor wastages in time and material may spell the difference between "breaking even" and showing a profit. Inefficient shop practices under poor management are often the cause of losses at the end of what has seemed to be a busy year.

When the salesman brings in a new job, the production manager should study and consider every phase of the work the job entails, and visualize the attendant problems. After he assigns the preparation of the stencils to the stencil department, the production

FIG. 120. View of cutting department with power cutter which may be set for varied automatic adjustments.

man should check with his assistant on his inventory of stock, paint and other related supplies, so that orders may be placed for the needed material in time for everything to be on hand when printing operations are scheduled to begin. Frequently, stock must be ordered well in advance, particularly paper of odd size or special weight or colors.

The wide-awake manager will so arrange his schedule, equipment, supplies and assignments as to eliminate all potential bottlenecks in the flow of production. The foreman or manager should assign a *specific* job to each person, who will be charged with a specific responsibility.

A wide delegation of work is the basis of good organization. When the job is turned over to the printing department, colors

FIG. 121. Assembly and packing department.

should be all ready—matched, mixed and proofed, a tested make-ready prepared, and a few prints pulled for checking. It is a waste of time to assemble the printing crew and make the men wait around listlessly while these preparations are being made. Often on complicated jobs, make-ready and proofing may take considerable time before the O.K. can be given to go ahead with the printing. There is nothing that kills efficiency and morale quite as much as to have men "hanging around" with folded arms because they have been called long before the work is ready for them. There is always some related productive work to be done, and it is the shop manager's job to anticipate every possible exigency. It is perverted economy to work with less help than you need. However, hiring more help than is essential impedes rather than helps production. They may be in each other's way.

Workers in the shop should be cautioned against smoking while at work, especially those whose work calls for repeated physical motions, such as are entailed in manual printing. The nature of such physical activity does not permit the leisurely demeanor of the habitual smoker. Puffing on a cigarette, then carefully balancing it on the edge of the table to keep an eye on it, then removing the ashes with the gesture of a country squire—these actions are definitely out of place in a busy shop. Not only does smoking tend to retard production, but it is an infringement of the law in the immediate proximity of inflammables. It endangers the lives of all.

A climate of efficiency and loyalty can be created for the employees by management's honest concern for their welfare as individuals, not merely as impersonal attendants of machines and equipment. Workers, even at the bottom rung in the hierarchy of skills, should be given an opportunity in some measure to participate in planning within their own sphere of activity. They should be encouraged to take a pride in their achievements, individually or collectively. Well-deserved praise is a wonderful tonic for fading spirits. Public reprimand, sarcasm, and abusive language will do inestimable damage to the worker's self-esteem and consequently will lower his morale, efficiency and loyalty. "Praise in public, criticize in private," is a wise adage.

22. ESTIMATING PROCEDURES

FOR A number of years a monthly article on estimating has been a regular feature of the industry's trade journal, *Screen Process Magazine*. The format of the article is as follows: A hypothetical "job" is set up with definite specifications as to quantity, size, number of colors, stock, etc. and the "specs" are sent out for bids among the nation-wide subscribers of the magazine. The results are then published in the form of a tabulated list of comparative estimates. The results? Prices may vary as much as three to one. For instance, the high rung on the ladder may be $1500, going down to a low of $500; yet all bidders apparently based their respective estimates on the identical set of specifications.

This great disparity is due to the fact that (discounting purely mathematical errors in computation) there appears to be no standard system of estimating for screen process.

No national fixed scale is easily established for an industry which is so geographically widespread and technically so vastly diversified. The costs that determine the final selling price vary in different parts of the country and often fluctuate even within a given locality. Each job, therefore, must be considered individually and estimated individually. To quote a fair and acceptable price on a proposed job, the salesman must actually look at and study the art from many points of view. To do this he must first of all be thoroughly acquainted with operating costs and production problems, as well as with the other less tangible factors that help form the basis of a reasonable estimate. This is a condition not quite duplicated in other graphic arts, such as letterpress and offset lithography. To present one major factor, say in the matter of cost of plates: In offset lithography, there is a fixed scale of prices for plates, based on the square inch. A 17" x 22" one-color plate will cost a definite amount (unless it entails some unusual problem) because the plate is produced photographically. A larger size plate will cost proportionately more. Not so in screen process. Since a good portion of stencils are hand cut, what matters is not how *large* the square *area* is, but what is *on* it. A 17" x 22" printing area may have only one word in it, or it may be loaded with small comp lettering rendered in pencil, and consequently requiring many hours of hand cutting.

Another reason why the screen process inherently resists price standardization is the versatility of materials and printing compounds associated with the process. Lithographers confine their work mostly to printing ink on paper. They can reasonably anticipate so many impressions per hour and can base their cost on that. Not quite so in screen process. Printing as it does, not only on paper, but on cardboard, metal, wood of varying sizes and thicknesses, no single rate-per-hour basis can apply to every case. It takes much more time and care to print on three-ply panel wood than it does on lightweight cardboard. In the last analysis, each job is individual and involves a certain amount of calculated guessing, along with sharpened-pencil mathematics.

The S.P.P.A. (Screen Process Printing Association, International) and local trade organizations have long endeavored to educate their constituents toward, not fixed, but *systematic* estimating procedures, with the hope that the glaring price disparities will be minimized. In this chapter, a general system of estimating is proposed to serve as a systematic guide, and yet be flexible enough to suit local needs and conditions.

PROPOSED SYSTEM OF ESTIMATING

Variable costs. Attempts have been made to help regulate prices within the law by standardizing at least one important factor in cost estimating: labor. However, since labor unions are more likely to exist in large cities, not all shops come under the jurisdiction of the unions.

There is also a great disparity in different sections of the country in the cost of rent, maintenance, insurance, local taxes, shipping and trucking, etc. Naturally, the selling price of a job will vary directly with the general basic costs; the higher the cost, the higher the price.

Competition. In figuring a price, not only the tangible costs but the more elusive factors, such as supply and demand, cannot be ignored. If on a given job, competition is usually keen, prices are apt to be pushed lower, although the operating costs remain the same. On a "first" job, representing the first time that the firm has been called in for a bid by a prospective client, some salesmen, in their desire to get an opening "wedge," are tempted to reduce the price somewhat in order to secure a new customer. This practice is ethically questionable, but it exists nonetheless.

Contractual work. The price charged for steady contract work, can, because it extends over a prescribed period, be lower than for an occasional individual job solicited in open competition. Work done on a long term basis offers many inherent advantages in economy, and therefore can be produced more cheaply. Because of the routinized experience and setup facilities for handling a given type of work, the price can be lowered, to the advantage of the client.

Seasonal work. During the "slow season" of the year, there are those who feel that even a minimum margin of profit is better than none at all, certainly better than having business at a standstill, with overhead costs continuing. As a general rule, it is wiser to retain the patronage of a wide clientele with a steady turnover of business at a nominal profit, than to limit the number of clients on a "charge as much as the traffic will bear" basis.

Nature of the job. A higher markup is justified and, in fact, necessary for the special responsibilities entailed in handling high calibre accounts. A fine concern will expect and gladly pay for quality printing to reflect its own high standards of craftsmanship or service. Because of the "extra" care required to produce a high quality job, screening expensive package designs for costly cosmetics will cost more than preparing "knockout" window posters advertising a local bargain sale.

In the final analysis, discretion and sound judgment begin where mathematics ends. Only seasoned experience will help the process

NO ______ SALESMAN'S INFORMATION DATE ______

SALESMAN ______ REPORT ______ INDUSTRY ______

FIRM ______ OLD ACC'T ______ NEW ACC'T ______
ADDRESS ______ CONTACTED BY TEL ___ PERSONAL CALL ______
TELEPHONE ______ DIRECT ACC'T ______ TRADE ______ C.B. ______
ADV. MGR. ______ WHEN WANTED ______ SALE ______ REJECTION ______
REMARKS ______

SUBJECT ______ DIE CUTTING ______ SIZE OF DIE ______
ART WORK ______ EASELING ______ SINGLE ___ DOUBLE ______
QUANTITY ______ SIZE OF EASEL ______ BOARD ______
SIZE ______ BEVELING ______
STOCK ______ COLOR ___ PT ___ BLEED ______ MOUNTING ______
COLORS ______ COVERAGE ___ BACKGROUND ______ FLOCKING ______ COLORS ______
LINES OF COPY ______ PACKED IN BULK ______
REGISTER ______ INDIVIDUAL CONTAINERS ___ #TO CONTAINER ______
VARNISHING ______ DELIVERY IN CITY ______ OUT OF CITY ______
SPECIAL MAKE READY ______ PROOF WANTED ______

INDIVIDUAL COLORS ROUGH SKETCH
1 ______
2 ______
3 ______
4 ______
5 ______
6 ______
7 ______
8 ______
9 ______
10 ______
11 ______
12 ______
13 ______
14 ______
15 ______

REPORT APPROVED BY ______ DATE ______
ESTIMATE MAILED ______ DATE ______
REMARKS ______

FIG. 122. Type of salesman's information sheet. (*Courtesy Paint Print Process, Inc., New York.*)

man interpret his local conditions and circumstances to determine the selling price.

ESTIMATING PROCEDURE

Collecting the facts. It is generally unwise to submit an estimate based merely on a verbal description of the job on the phone or in person. Such information is not always complete or accurate and does not form a sound basis for a definite estimate. The price you give may be either too high or too low. Somebody, either you or the customer, may be shortchanged. The best policy to follow, and one which will avoid subsequent misunderstanding, is to carefully study the actual finished art work that you· are asked to figure on. To prevent oversights in judgment or in incomplete data, it is best for the salesman to use a printed form on which to make a written record of all the facts pertinent to the proposed job.

Salesman's information sheets. The form shown in Figure 122, or a similar form, is a good device for recording data on jobs for later referral in figuring the estimate. It can be inserted in a handy loose-leaf binder and becomes a permanent record. The salesman, with the original art work before him, fills in the points of information called for in the printed sheet. If possible, too, a sketch or a Polaroid snapshot of the art should be attached to the form to serve as a visual reminder of the layout. Of course, discretion will dictate that the salesman obtain the client's permission to photograph the art.

Estimate sheet. With all the specifications on the salesman's information sheet taken into consideration, the expected costs are filled in on the estimate sheet. This sheet then becomes a record of estimated costs from which the selling price is computed. In Figure 123 note the column labeled "Cost" (third column from the left). This lists the *estimated* cost of all that goes into production. The column headed "Actual Cost" is computed when the job is finished. After the job is completed, both these columns are then compared to see how close the estimated cost approaches the actual cost. Any great disparity between these two would in-

No _____	ESTIMATE SHEET		Date _____

INDUSTRY _____ SALESMAN _____ COMMISSION _____
FIRM _____ Old Acc't _____ New Acc't _____
Address _____ Contacted by Tel _____ Personal Call _____
Telephone _____ Direct Acc't ____ Trade _____ C.B. _____
Adv. Mgr. _____ When Wanted _____
Remarks _____

SCREEN PRINTING	QUANTITY	COST	TOTAL	ACTUAL COST
SUBJECT				
ART WORK				
SIZE				
STOCK COLOR PT. BLEED				
MAKE READY				
PAINT				
VARNISH				
LABOR CREW				
HANDLING				
TRUCKING				
MOUNTING AND FINISHING				
MOUNTING TRIMMING				
DIE				
DIE CUTTING				
EASEL SIZE CHIP JUTE				
EASELING				
PACKING				
CONTAINERS				
SHIPPING				
SPECIAL TREATMENT				
BEVELING				
HAND WORK				
FLOCK				
FLOCKING				
PROOF WANTED				
TOTAL MFG. COST				
TOTAL				
MARK UP				
SELLING PRICE				
UNIT PRICE				

O.K'D. BY _____

REMARKS _____

FIG. 123. Estimate sheet. (*Courtesy Paint Print Process, Inc., New York.*)

dicate bad arithmetic or poor judgment somewhere along the line. Such a study will serve as guidance for the future.

Estimate confirmation sheet. Most clients expect a written confirmation of quotations to prevent misunderstandings, squabbles and litigations. Even if the customer does not request a written estimate, it is good business practice to send him a written esti-

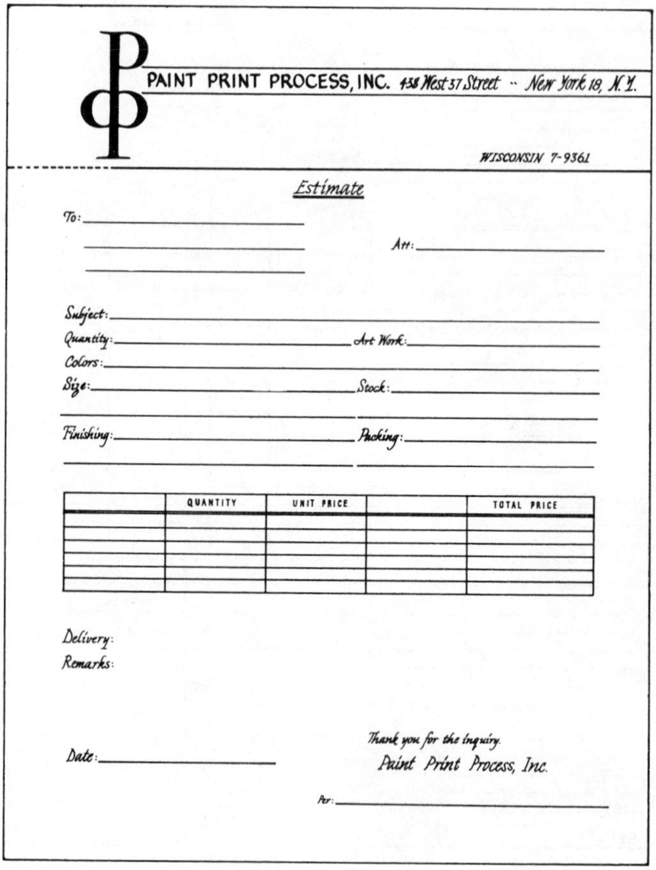

PAINT PRINT PROCESS, INC. 438 West 37 Street - New York 18, N.Y.

WISCONSIN 7-9361

Estimate

To:

Att:

Subject:

Quantity: Art Work:

Colors:

Size: Stock:

Finishing: Packing:

	QUANTITY	UNIT PRICE		TOTAL PRICE

Delivery:

Remarks:

Date:

Thank you for the inquiry.

Paint Print Process, Inc.

Per:

FIG. 124. Estimate confirmation sheet. (*Courtesy Paint Print Process, Inc., New York.*)

mate as a matter of routine procedure. This should, of course, be in duplicate: the customer gets a copy, you keep a copy.

Instead of composing a letter in prose form for each quotation, a confirmation sheet such as the one shown in Figure 124 will be expedient, to the point, easy to fill out and easy to read. It will serve as a document bearing the vendor's name, all the specifications, and the signature of the person authorized to quote the job.

Figuring the job. The general anatomy of the estimating

structure is composed of three main areas: (1) Material costs (2) Labor costs (3) Overhead costs. These can be further subdivided into various related categories depending upon bookkeeping requirements.

1. Material costs include:

(a) Stock. The material on which the printing is done, such as paper, cardboard, vinyl sheets, etc.

(b) Printing compounds. The paint, enamel, lacquer, or whatever is used in printing.

(c) Stencil making medium. Materials needed to prepare the stencils, such as film, photographic chemicals, fill-in lacquer, etc.

(d) Finishing. This includes the die cutter's charges for die cutting, easeling, laminating, etc.

(e) Shipping. This includes the cost of special containers, shipping cases, trucking, etc.

(f) Miscellaneous. Cost of outside-produced art work, construction models, and other out-of-pocket expenditures.

In general, the material cost represents a total of all out-of-pocket expenditures necessary to produce the job.

To cover these costs plus a margin for handling, possible waste, etc. a markup of fifteen percent is added. Thus, if the anticipated cost for materials is $1000, it will be computed at $1150.

2. Labor costs include:

(a) Art work. The cost of art work produced by the shop's art staff. It includes preliminary sketches, models, finished art, revisions, etc.

(b) Color mixing. This charge is based on the time it takes to match, mix and proof colors.

(c) Make-ready. The cost of getting the screen ready, setting guides, checking register and running pre-production color proofs.

(d) Stencil making. This charge is based on the time it takes to plan and prepare the series of stencils.

(e) Printing. This charge is based on the time it takes to print the entire job.

(f) Handling. This charge is based on the man-hours it takes to handle the stock from the time it is delivered from the supplier to the time the finished job is ready for shipping.

(g) Supervision. A charge for the production manager or foreman's time prorated for the particular job.

Seventy-five percent is added to the total labor costs. Thus, if the total labor cost figures $1000, it will be computed as $1750.

3. Overhead includes:

(a) Rent.

(b) Utilities. Telephone, electricity, power, gas, etc.

(c) Depreciation. Prorated wear and tear on production equipment. Maintenance and repair.

(d) Taxes. Local and federal taxes.

(e) Miscellaneous. This includes trade and labor organiza- tion dues, employees' compensation expenses, employees' vacation money, bookkeeping, insurance, stationery sup- plies, promotion, bad debts, etc.

From the total yearly overhead costs, it is a matter of mathe- matics to compute the daily overhead per working day, arriving at an average figure of so much per work day. This is computed on the anticipated number of days it will take one crew (generally a team of two people) to do the job. There is usually no markup on the overhead costs.

A hypothetical estimate follows:

Material costs:	$1000 + 15% ($1000 + $150).	$1150.00
Labor costs:	$1000 + 75% ($1000 + $750).	$1750.00
Overhead (Prorated at $50 a day—4 days).		$ 200.00

$3100.00

To this add a 10% salesman's commission   310.00
   (even if you are your own salesman)
                                   Total $3410.00

The above example may appear as an oversimplification of a more involved accounting structure. It is intended, however, merely to serve as a basis for a system of estimating and is subject to variations. The point made here is that the processor must develop some basic pattern for mathematically determining the final selling price, and the figuring should not be done "in the head," but on paper, in an organized, consistent manner.

23. SOURCES OF SUPPLY

THE FOLLOWING listing by no means presumes to be a complete directory of manufacturers or dealers of screen process materials. Rather, it is merely a sampling of firms whose consistent advertisements in *Screen Process Magazine* and other trade journals have made their names, products and services widely known in the trade.

The list does not include the roster of the literally hundreds of individual art stores and local dealers throughout the country who carry silk screen supplies and accessories. These you will find listed in your local phone book directory under such variable headings as:

Silk Screen Process Supplies
Screen Process Supplies
Art Supplies
Sign Supplies
Graphic Art Supplies

Advance Process Supply Company, Inc., 400 N. Noble, Chicago, Illinois 60622. Press equipment and related supplies.

Albert Godde Bedin, Inc., 111 Calumet Street, Depew, New York 14042. Screen fabrics.

Alphatype Corporation, 7500 McCormick Blvd., Skokie, Illinois 60076. Photo-lettering machines and related products.

American Screen Printing Equipment Company, 404 N. Noble, Chicago, Illinois 60622. Press equipment and supplies.

Atlas Silk Screen Company, 1733 Milwaukee Ave., Chicago, Illinois 60647. Press equipment and supplies.

Becker Sign Supply Company, 319-321 N. Paca St., Baltimore, Maryland 21201. General supplies.

Bourges Color Corporation, 20 Waterside Plaza, New York, New York 10010. Bourges color sheets and related supplies.

Cello-Tak Manufacturing, Inc., 35 Alabama Ave., Island Park, Long Island, New York 11558. Transfer type and shading sheets.

Cincinnati Silk Screen Process Supplies, Inc., 420 Commercial Square, Cincinnati, Ohio 45202. Drying ovens and related products.

Claremont Flock Corporation, Main Street, P. O. Box 451, Claremont, New Hampshire 03743. Flock material.

Coating Products, Inc., 580 Sylvan Ave., Englewood Cliffs, New Jersey 07632. Pressure-sensitive materials and metalized plastics.

Colonial Process Supply Company, 180 E. Union Ave., East Rutherford, New Jersey 07073. General supplies.

Craftint Manufacturing Company, 18501 Euclid Ave., Cleveland, Ohio 44112. Paints, shading sheets and related products.

Cudner and O'Connor Company, 4035 W. Kinzie St., Chicago, Illinois 60624. Lacquer and plastic inks.

Day-Glo Color Corporation, 4732 St. Clair Ave., Cleveland, Ohio 44103. Fluorescent paints and related products.

E. I. du Pont de Nemours & Company, Inc., 2420-17 Nemours Building, Wilmington, Delaware 19898. Photo films and related supplies.

Eastman Kodak Company, 343 State Street, Rochester, New York 14650. Photo films and related supplies.

Excello Color & Chemical Corporation, 400 N. Noble, Chicago, Illinois 60622. Paints.

Fasson, Division Avery Products Corporation, 250 Chester St., Painesville, Ohio 44077. Self-adhesive materials.

Fostoria Industries, Inc., 1200 N. Main St., P. O. Box E, Fostoria, Ohio 44830. Infra-red drying systems.

General Research, Inc., 309 S. Union, Sparta, Michigan 49345. Presses and driers, related equipment.

Glidden-Durkee, Division of SCM Corporation, Union Commerce Bldg., Cleveland, Ohio 44102. Paints and related supplies.

Graphic Equipment of Boston, Inc., 1217 Hyde Park Ave., Hyde, Boston, Massachusetts 02120. Presses and related equipment.

Griffin Manufacturing Company, 1658 Ridge Road, East Webster, New York 14580. Stencil knives and related instruments.

O. Hommel Company, Hope and Maple Streets, Carnegie, Pennsylvania 15106. Ceramic colors.

Iddings Paint Company, Inc., 45-30 38th St., Long Island City, New York 11101. Water-base paints.

Inmont Corporation, 1133 Ave. of the Americas, New York, New York 10036. Paints and related products.

Lawson Printing Machine Company, 4434 Olive St., St. Louis, Missouri 63108. Printing equipment.

Kenro Graphics, Inc., Cedar Knolls, New Jersey 07927. Cameras and related products.

McGraw Colorgraphic Company, 175 W. Verdugo Ave., Burbank, California 91506. Photo films and related supplies.

McLogan Supply Co., Inc., 1324 S. Hope St., Los Angeles, California 90015. General supplies.

The Mearl Company, 41 E. 42nd St., New York, New York 10017. Lustrous synthetic pearl essence.

Medalist, M & M Research and Printing Aids, 13111 W. Silver Spring Dr., P.O. Box 615, Butler, Wisconsin 53007. Presses and related equipment.

Minnesota Mining and Manufacturing Company (3M Center), Decorative Products Division, 2501 Hudson Rd., St. Paul, Minnesota 55101. Reflective films, non-reflective films, woodgrain films, and related products.

Naz-Dar Company, 1087 N. Branch, Chicago, Illinois 60622. Paints and general supplies.

Nu Arc Company, Inc., 4100 W. Grand Ave., Chicago, Illinois 60651. Photo equipment.

Nu-film Products Company, Inc., 56 W. 22nd St., New York, New York 10010. General supplies and stencil film.

Permafrost Corporation, 22 Fairfield Place, West Caldwell, New Jersey 07006. Tinsel, glitter and related products.

Protype Inc., 89 W. 3rd St., New York, New York 10012. Photo-lettering equipment.

Joseph E. Podgor Company, Inc., 7895 Browning Road, Pennsauken, New Jersey 08109. General supplies.

Precision Screen Machines Company, Inc., 44 Utter Ave., Hawthorne, New Jersey 07506. Presses and related equipment.

Process Camera & Equipment, Inc., 935 N. Damen, Chicago, Illinois 60622. Cameras and related supplies.

Radiant Color Company, 2800 Radiant Ave., Richmond, California 94804. Fluorescent colors and related products.

Roberts & Porter, Inc., 49-16 Newton Road, Long Island City, New York 11103. Photo films and related supplies.

Serascreen Corporation, 5-25 47th Road, Long Island City, New York 11101. General supplies and equipment.

Sherwin-Williams, 101 Prospect NW, Cleveland, Ohio 44101. Paints and related products.

Sinclair and Valentine Company, Box 1167, Secaucus Rd., Secaucus, New Jersey 07094. Paints and related products.

Tibbetts-Westerfield Screen Process Supply Company, 2600 E. 8th St., Los Angeles, California 90023. Decal paper and supplies.

Ulano Companies, 210 E. 86th St., New York, New York 10028. Stencil films and related supplies.

Union Ink Company, Inc., 453 Broad Ave., Ridgefield, New Jersey 07657; 2310 Lodi St., Syracuse, New York 13208. Paints and related products.

Martin J. Weber Process, 171 Madison Ave., New York, New York 10016. Preparation of posterized film positives for silk screen.

Western Supply Company, Inc., 2525 W. Washington Blvd., Los Angeles, California 90018. General screen supplies

Willmann Paper Company, 405 Hudson St., New York, New York 10014. Paper and board.

Wornow Products, Department Hysol, Division of the Dexter Corp., 15051 E. Don Julian Rd., City of Industry, California 91749. Screen printing paints and inks.

24. BIBLIOGRAPHY

THIS IS not an extensive bibliography. Very little has been written on the process prior to 1926, when Harry L. Hiett's *Manual on Stencil Screen Process Work, Formulas, Working Instructions, and General Up to Date Information* came out, published by the author. The book not only had a long title, but had a long publishing life. It is out of print now. This was followed by Bert Zahn's *Silk Screen Methods of Reproduction,* published in 1935.

Listed below are active books on the screen process.

Biegeleisen, J. I., *Silk Screen Stencil Craft as a Hobby,* New York, Harper and Brothers, 1935. Deals with the craft and hobby aspects of the process. It is now out of print but in circulation in some libraries.

Biegeleisen, J. I., and Cohn, M. A., *Silk Screen Techniques,* New York, Dover Publications, 1958. Deals with all the major processes and techniques of silk screen printing. Emphasis, however, is on the fine arts aspect of the process, known as serigraphy.

Carr, Frances, *Guide to Screen Process Printing,* New York, Pitman Publishing Corp., 1962. General treatment of the subject.

Darby, Sidney, *Screen Process Printing*, Scranton, Pa., International Correspondence Schools. A short (85-page) treatise on the fundamentals of the process.

Eisenberg and Kafka, *Silk Screen Printing,* Bloomington, Ill., McKnight & McKnight Publishing Co., 1957. A general treatment of the subject.

Fossett, Robert O., *Techniques in Photography for the Silk Screen Printer,* Cincinnati, Ohio, Signs of the Times Publishing Company, 1959. An excellent treatment of the various photographic procedures for preparing photographic stencils.

Harkins, Dorothy, *Screening Fabric Techniques.* One of the few books on this phase of the process.

Hiett, Harry L., *Screen Process Production,* Cincinnati, Ohio, Signs of the Times Publishing Co., 1936. A basic book, now out of print.

Kosloff, Albert, *Ceramic Screen Printing,* Cincinnati, Ohio, Signs of the Times Publishing Co., 1962. A good source of information on the subject.

Kosloff, Albert, *Photographic Screen Process Printing,* Cincinnati, Ohio, Signs of the Times Publishing Co. An excellent companion piece to Fossett's book on the same subject.

Kosloff, Albert, *Screen Process Printing,* Cincinnati, Ohio, Signs of the Times Publishing Co., 1950. A good, all-around book on the process.

Mytton-Davies, Peter, *Screen Process Printing,* Middlesex, England, Press and Process Publications, 1952. A survey of the process as it is practiced in Great Britain.

Shokler, Harry, *Artist's Manual for Silk Screen Print Making,* New York, Tudor Publications, 1960. A good book on the process written by a fine art practitioner in the field.

Sternberg, Harry, *Silk Screen Color Printing,* New York, McGraw-Hill Book Company, 1942. An excellent book limited primarily to the tusche method of stencil making.

Zahn, Bert, *Silk Screen Methods of Reproduction,* Wilmette, Illinois, Frederick J. Drake & Company, 1950. A basic, authoritative book written by one of the industry's pioneers in the process.

The authoritative trade journal for the process industry is *Screen Process Magazine,* published monthly by the Signs of the Times Publishing Company, 407 Gilbert Avenue, Cincinnati, Ohio. This periodical features articles by the experts in the various ramifications of the process. It is also an important vehicle for learning about suppliers and their products through their ads.

The companion magazine to *Screen Process* is the monthly journal, *Signs of the Times.* Though this deals primarily with sign craft, there are many overlapping areas in process work. It is published by the same publisher as *Screen Process Magazine.*

Display World, also a Signs of the Times periodical, treats the developments in the field of merchandising, displays and point-of-sale advertising.

In addition to the above, most graphic arts magazines carry occasional stories and features on the process. One of these magazines is *Graphic Arts Monthly,* published by the Graphic Arts Publication Company, 608 S. Dearborn Street, Chicago 5, Ill.

The S.P.P.A. Int. (Screen Process Printing Association International) published in 1954 a manual prepared by its Vocational Development Committee. This is a brief survey of the process, materials, techniques, etc.

The S.P.P.A. has also collated data of tremendous value to the processor. A virtual treasure-chest of information is published and distributed to members of the Association. Additional segments are mailed periodically to the interested in a loose-leaf binder made for the purpose. This is the Association's *Manual for Screen Process Printers.* The S.P.P.A.'s address is 549 West Randolph Street, Chicago 6, Illinois.

INDEX

A CATALOGUE OF SELECTED DOVER BOOKS
IN ALL FIELDS OF INTEREST

A CATALOGUE OF SELECTED DOVER
BOOKS IN ALL FIELDS OF INTEREST

CELESTIAL OBJECTS FOR COMMON TELESCOPES, T. W. Webb. The most used book in amateur astronomy: inestimable aid for locating and identifying nearly 4,000 celestial objects. Edited, updated by Margaret W. Mayall. 77 illustrations. Total of 645pp. 5⅜ x 8½.
20917-2, 20918-0 Pa., Two-vol. set $9.00

HISTORICAL STUDIES IN THE LANGUAGE OF CHEMISTRY, M. P. Crosland. The important part language has played in the development of chemistry from the symbolism of alchemy to the adoption of systematic nomenclature in 1892. ". . . wholeheartedly recommended,"—Science. 15 illustrations. 416pp. of text. 5⅝ x 8¼.
63702-6 Pa. $6.00

BURNHAM'S CELESTIAL HANDBOOK, Robert Burnham, Jr. Thorough, readable guide to the stars beyond our solar system. Exhaustive treatment, fully illustrated. Breakdown is alphabetical by constellation: Andromeda to Cetus in Vol. 1; Chamaeleon to Orion in Vol. 2; and Pavo to Vulpecula in Vol. 3. Hundreds of illustrations. Total of about 2000pp. 6⅛ x 9¼.
23567-X, 23568-8, 23673-0 Pa., Three-vol. set $27.85

THEORY OF WING SECTIONS: INCLUDING A SUMMARY OF AIR-FOIL DATA, Ira H. Abbott and A. E. von Doenhoff. Concise compilation of subatomic aerodynamic characteristics of modern NASA wing sections, plus description of theory. 350pp. of tables. 693pp. 5⅜ x 8½.
60586-8 Pa. $8.50

DE RE METALLICA, Georgius Agricola. Translated by Herbert C. Hoover and Lou H. Hoover. The famous Hoover translation of greatest treatise on technological chemistry, engineering, geology, mining of early modern times (1556). All 289 original woodcuts. 638pp. 6¾ x 11.
60006-8 Clothbd. $17.95

THE ORIGIN OF CONTINENTS AND OCEANS, Alfred Wegener. One of the most influential, most controversial books in science, the classic statement for continental drift. Full 1966 translation of Wegener's final (1929) version. 64 illustrations. 246pp. 5⅜ x 8½.
61708-4 Pa. $4.50

THE PRINCIPLES OF PSYCHOLOGY, William James. Famous long course complete, unabridged. Stream of thought, time perception, memory, experimental methods; great work decades ahead of its time. Still valid, useful; read in many classes. 94 figures. Total of 1391pp. 5⅜ x 8½.
20381-6, 20382-4 Pa., Two-vol. set $13.00

THE COMPLETE BOOK OF DOLL MAKING AND COLLECTING, Catherine Christopher. Instructions, patterns for dozens of dolls, from rag doll on up to elaborate, historically accurate figures. Mould faces, sew clothing, make doll houses, etc. Also collecting information. Many illustrations. 288pp. 6 x 9. 22066-4 Pa. $4.50

THE DAGUERREOTYPE IN AMERICA, Beaumont Newhall. Wonderful portraits, 1850's townscapes, landscapes; full text plus 104 photographs. The basic book. Enlarged 1976 edition. 272pp. 8¼ x 11¼. 23322-7 Pa. $7.95

CRAFTSMAN HOMES, Gustav Stickley. 296 architectural drawings, floor plans, and photographs illustrate 40 different kinds of "Mission-style" homes from *The Craftsman* (1901-16), voice of American style of simplicity and organic harmony. Thorough coverage of Craftsman idea in text and picture, now collector's item. 224pp. 8⅛ x 11. 23791-5 Pa. $6.00

PEWTER-WORKING: INSTRUCTIONS AND PROJECTS, Burl N. Osborn. & Gordon O. Wilber. Introduction to pewter-working for amateur craftsman. History and characteristics of pewter; tools, materials, step-by-step instructions. Photos, line drawings, diagrams. Total of 160pp. 7⅞ x 10¾. 23786-9 Pa. $3.50

THE GREAT CHICAGO FIRE, edited by David Lowe. 10 dramatic, eyewitness accounts of the 1871 disaster, including one of the aftermath and rebuilding, plus 70 contemporary photographs and illustrations of the ruins—courthouse, Palmer House, Great Central Depot, etc. Introduction by David Lowe. 87pp. 8¼ x 11. 23771-0 Pa. $4.00

SILHOUETTES: A PICTORIAL ARCHIVE OF VARIED ILLUSTRATIONS, edited by Carol Belanger Grafton. Over 600 silhouettes from the 18th to 20th centuries include profiles and full figures of men and women, children, birds and animals, groups and scenes, nature, ships, an alphabet. Dozens of uses for commercial artists and craftspeople. 144pp. 8⅜ x 11¼. 23781-8 Pa. $4.50

ANIMALS: 1,419 COPYRIGHT-FREE ILLUSTRATIONS OF MAMMALS, BIRDS, FISH, INSECTS, ETC., edited by Jim Harter. Clear wood engravings present, in extremely lifelike poses, over 1,000 species of animals. One of the most extensive copyright-free pictorial sourcebooks of its kind. Captions. Index. 284pp. 9 x 12. 23766-4 Pa. $8.95

INDIAN DESIGNS FROM ANCIENT ECUADOR, Frederick W. Shaffer. 282 original designs by pre-Columbian Indians of Ecuador (500-1500 A.D.). Designs include people, mammals, birds, reptiles, fish, plants, heads, geometric designs. Use as is or alter for advertising, textiles, leathercraft, etc. Introduction. 95pp. 8¾ x 11¼. 23764-8 Pa. $3.50

SZIGETI ON THE VIOLIN, Joseph Szigeti. Genial, loosely structured tour by premier violinist, featuring a pleasant mixture of reminiscences, insights into great music and musicians, innumerable tips for practicing violinists. 385 musical passages. 256pp. 5⅝ x 8¼. 23763-X Pa. $4.00

AMERICAN BIRD ENGRAVINGS, Alexander Wilson et al. All 76 plates. from Wilson's *American Ornithology* (1808-14), most important ornithological work before Audubon, plus 27 plates from the supplement (1825-33) by Charles Bonaparte. Over 250 birds portrayed. 8 plates also reproduced in full color. 111pp. 9⅜ x 12½.   23195-X Pa. $6.00

CRUICKSHANK'S PHOTOGRAPHS OF BIRDS OF AMERICA, Allan D. Cruickshank. Great ornithologist, photographer presents 177 closeups, groupings, panoramas, flightings, etc., of about 150 different birds. Expanded *Wings in the Wilderness*. Introduction by Helen G. Cruickshank. 191pp. 8¼ x 11.   23497-5 Pa. $6.00

AMERICAN WILDLIFE AND PLANTS, A. C. Martin, et al. Describes food habits of more than 1000 species of mammals, birds, fish. Special treatment of important food plants. Over 300 illustrations. 500pp. 5⅜ x 8½.
20793-5 Pa. $4.95

THE PEOPLE CALLED SHAKERS, Edward D. Andrews. Lifetime of research, definitive study of Shakers: origins, beliefs, practices, dances, social organization, furniture and crafts, impact on 19th-century USA, present heritage. Indispensable to student of American history, collector. 33 illustrations. 351pp. 5⅜ x 8½.   21081-2 Pa. $4.50

OLD NEW YORK IN EARLY PHOTOGRAPHS, Mary Black. New York City as it was in 1853-1901, through 196 wonderful photographs from N.-Y. Historical Society. Great Blizzard, Lincoln's funeral procession, great buildings. 228pp. 9 x 12.   22907-6 Pa. $8.95

MR. LINCOLN'S CAMERA MAN: MATHEW BRADY, Roy Meredith. Over 300 Brady photos reproduced directly from original negatives, photos. Jackson, Webster, Grant, Lee, Carnegie, Barnum; Lincoln; Battle Smoke, Death of Rebel Sniper, Atlanta Just After Capture. Lively commentary. 368pp. 8⅜ x 11¼.   23021-X Pa. $8.95

TRAVELS OF WILLIAM BARTRAM, William Bartram. From 1773-8, Bartram explored Northern Florida, Georgia, Carolinas, and reported on wild life, plants, Indians, early settlers. Basic account for period, entertaining reading. Edited by Mark Van Doren. 13 illustrations. 141pp. 5⅜ x 8½.   20013-2 Pa. $5.00

THE GENTLEMAN AND CABINET MAKER'S DIRECTOR, Thomas Chippendale. Full reprint, 1762 style book, most influential of all time; chairs, tables, sofas, mirrors, cabinets, etc. 200 plates, plus 24 photographs of surviving pieces. 249pp. 9⅞ x 12¾.   21601-2 Pa. $7.95

AMERICAN CARRIAGES, SLEIGHS, SULKIES AND CARTS, edited by Don H. Berkebile. 168 Victorian illustrations from catalogues, trade journals, fully captioned. Useful for artists. Author is Assoc. Curator, Div. of Transportation of Smithsonian Institution. 168pp. 8½ x 9½.
23328-6 Pa. $5.00

THE PHILOSOPHY OF HISTORY, Georg W. Hegel. Great classic of Western thought develops concept that history is not chance but a rational process, the evolution of freedom. 457pp. 5⅜ x 8½.   20112-0 Pa. $4.50

LANGUAGE, TRUTH AND LOGIC, Alfred J. Ayer. Famous, clear introduction to Vienna, Cambridge schools of Logical Positivism. Role of philosophy, elimination of metaphysics, nature of analysis, etc. 160pp. 5⅜ x 8½. (Available in U.S. only)   20010-8 Pa. $2.00

A PREFACE TO LOGIC, Morris R. Cohen. Great City College teacher in renowned, easily followed exposition of formal logic, probability, values, logic and world order and similar topics; no previous background needed. 209pp. 5⅜ x 8½.   23517-3 Pa. $3.50

REASON AND NATURE, Morris R. Cohen. Brilliant analysis of reason and its multitudinous ramifications by charismatic teacher. Interdisciplinary, synthesizing work widely praised when it first appeared in 1931. Second (1953) edition. Indexes. 496pp. 5⅜ x 8½.   23633-1 Pa. $6.50

AN ESSAY CONCERNING HUMAN UNDERSTANDING, John Locke. The only complete edition of enormously important classic, with authoritative editorial material by A. C. Fraser. Total of 1176pp. 5⅜ x 8½.
20530-4, 20531-2 Pa., Two-vol. set $16.00

HANDBOOK OF MATHEMATICAL FUNCTIONS WITH FORMULAS, GRAPHS, AND MATHEMATICAL TABLES, edited by Milton Abramowitz and Irene A. Stegun. Vast compendium: 29 sets of tables, some to as high as 20 places. 1,046pp. 8 x 10½.   61272-4 Pa. $14.95

MATHEMATICS FOR THE PHYSICAL SCIENCES, Herbert S. Wilf. Highly acclaimed work offers clear presentations of vector spaces and matrices, orthogonal functions, roots of polynomial equations, conformal mapping, calculus of variations, etc. Knowledge of theory of functions of real and complex variables is assumed. Exercises and solutions. Index. 284pp. 5⅝ x 8¼.   63635-6 Pa. $5.00

THE PRINCIPLE OF RELATIVITY, Albert Einstein et al. Eleven most important original papers on special and general theories. Seven by Einstein, two by Lorentz, one each by Minkowski and Weyl. All translated, unabridged. 216pp. 5⅜ x 8½.   60081-5 Pa. $3.50

THERMODYNAMICS, Enrico Fermi. A classic of modern science. Clear, organized treatment of systems, first and second laws, entropy, thermodynamic potentials, gaseous reactions, dilute solutions, entropy constant. No math beyond calculus required. Problems. 160pp. 5⅜ x 8½.
60361-X Pa. $3.00

ELEMENTARY MECHANICS OF FLUIDS, Hunter Rouse. Classic undergraduate text widely considered to be far better than many later books. Ranges from fluid velocity and acceleration to role of compressibility in fluid motion. Numerous examples, questions, problems. 224 illustrations. 376pp. 5⅝ x 8¼.   63699-2 Pa. $5.00

ART FORMS IN NATURE, Ernst Haeckel. Multitude of strangely beautiful natural forms: Radiolaria, Foraminifera, jellyfishes, fungi, turtles, bats, etc. All 100 plates of the 19th-century evolutionist's *Kunstformen der Natur* (1904). 100pp. 9⅜ x 12¼. 22987-4 Pa. $5.00

CHILDREN: A PICTORIAL ARCHIVE FROM NINETEENTH-CENTURY SOURCES, edited by Carol Belanger Grafton. 242 rare, copyright-free wood engravings for artists and designers. Widest such selection available. All illustrations in line. 119pp. 8⅜ x 11¼. 23694-3 Pa. $4.00

WOMEN: A PICTORIAL ARCHIVE FROM NINETEENTH-CENTURY SOURCES, edited by Jim Harter. 391 copyright-free wood engravings for artists and designers selected from rare periodicals. Most extensive such collection available. All illustrations in line. 128pp. 9 x 12. 23703-6 Pa. $4.50

ARABIC ART IN COLOR, Prisse d'Avennes. From the greatest ornamentalists of all time—50 plates in color, rarely seen outside the Near East, rich in suggestion and stimulus. Includes 4 plates on covers. 46pp. 9⅜ x 12¼. 23658-7 Pa. $6.00

AUTHENTIC ALGERIAN CARPET DESIGNS AND MOTIFS, edited by June Beveridge. Algerian carpets are world famous. Dozens of geometrical motifs are charted on grids, color-coded, for weavers, needleworkers, craftsmen, designers. 53 illustrations plus 4 in color. 48pp. 8¼ x 11. (Available in U.S. only) 23650-1 Pa. $1.75

DICTIONARY OF AMERICAN PORTRAITS, edited by Hayward and Blanche Cirker. 4000 important Americans, earliest times to 1905, mostly in clear line. Politicians, writers, soldiers, scientists, inventors, industrialists, Indians, Blacks, women, outlaws, etc. Identificatory information. 756pp. 9¼ x 12¾. 21823-6 Clothbd. $40.00

HOW THE OTHER HALF LIVES, Jacob A. Riis. Journalistic record of filth, degradation, upward drive in New York immigrant slums, shops, around 1900. New edition includes 100 original Riis photos, monuments of early photography. 233pp. 10 x 7⅞. 22012-5 Pa. $7.00

NEW YORK IN THE THIRTIES, Berenice Abbott. Noted photographer's fascinating study of city shows new buildings that have become famous and old sights that have disappeared forever. Insightful commentary. 97 photographs. 97pp. 11⅜ x 10. 22967-X Pa. $5.00

MEN AT WORK, Lewis W. Hine. Famous photographic studies of construction workers, railroad men, factory workers and coal miners. New supplement of 18 photos on Empire State building construction. New introduction by Jonathan L. Doherty. Total of 69 photos. 63pp. 8 x 10¾. 23475-4 Pa. $3.00

YUCATAN BEFORE AND AFTER THE CONQUEST, Diego de Landa. First English translation of basic book in Maya studies, the only significant account of Yucatan written in the early post-Conquest era. Translated by distinguished Maya scholar William Gates. Appendices, introduction, 4 maps and over 120 illustrations added by translator. 162pp. 5⅜ x 8½.
23622-6 Pa. $3.00

THE MALAY ARCHIPELAGO, Alfred R. Wallace. Spirited travel account by one of founders of modern biology. Touches on zoology, botany, ethnography, geography, and geology. 62 illustrations, maps. 515pp. 5⅜ x 8½.
20187-2 Pa. $6.95

THE DISCOVERY OF THE TOMB OF TUTANKHAMEN, Howard Carter, A. C. Mace. Accompany Carter in the thrill of discovery, as ruined passage suddenly reveals unique, untouched, fabulously rich tomb. Fascinating account, with 106 illustrations. New introduction by J. M. White. Total of 382pp. 5⅜ x 8½. (Available in U.S. only)   23500-9 Pa. $4.00

THE WORLD'S GREATEST SPEECHES, edited by Lewis Copeland and Lawrence W. Lamm. Vast collection of 278 speeches from Greeks up to present. Powerful and effective models; unique look at history. Revised to 1970. Indices. 842pp. 5⅜ x 8½.   20468-5 Pa. $8.95

THE 100 GREATEST ADVERTISEMENTS, Julian Watkins. The priceless ingredient; His master's voice; 99 44/100% pure; over 100 others. How they were written, their impact, etc. Remarkable record. 130 illustrations. 233pp. 7⅞ x 10 3/5.   20540-1 Pa. $5.95

CRUICKSHANK PRINTS FOR HAND COLORING, George Cruickshank. 18 illustrations, one side of a page, on fine-quality paper suitable for watercolors. Caricatures of people in society (c. 1820) full of trenchant wit. Very large format. 32pp. 11 x 16.   23684-6 Pa. $5.00

THIRTY-TWO COLOR POSTCARDS OF TWENTIETH-CENTURY AMERICAN ART, Whitney Museum of American Art. Reproduced in full color in postcard form are 31 art works and one shot of the museum. Calder, Hopper, Rauschenberg, others. Detachable. 16pp. 8¼ x 11.
23629-3 Pa. $3.00

MUSIC OF THE SPHERES: THE MATERIAL UNIVERSE FROM ATOM TO QUASAR SIMPLY EXPLAINED, Guy Murchie. Planets, stars, geology, atoms, radiation, relativity, quantum theory, light, antimatter, similar topics. 319 figures. 664pp. 5⅜ x 8½.
21809-0, 21810-4 Pa., Two-vol. set $11.00

EINSTEIN'S THEORY OF RELATIVITY, Max Born. Finest semi-technical account; covers Einstein, Lorentz, Minkowski, and others, with much detail, much explanation of ideas and math not readily available elsewhere on this level. For student, non-specialist. 376pp. 5⅜ x 8½.
60769-0 Pa. $4.50

DRAWINGS OF WILLIAM BLAKE, William Blake. 92 plates from Book of Job, *Divine Comedy, Paradise Lost,* visionary heads, mythological figures, Laocoon, etc. Selection, introduction, commentary by Sir Geoffrey Keynes. 178pp. 8⅛ x 11. 22303-5 Pa. $4.00

ENGRAVINGS OF HOGARTH, William Hogarth. 101 of Hogarth's greatest works: *Rake's Progress, Harlot's Progress, Illustrations for Hudibras, Before and After, Beer Street and Gin Lane,* many more. Full commentary. 256pp. 11 x 13¾. 22479-1 Pa. $12.95

DAUMIER: 120 GREAT LITHOGRAPHS, Honore Daumier. Wide-ranging collection of lithographs by the greatest caricaturist of the 19th century. Concentrates on eternally popular series on lawyers, on married life, on liberated women, etc. Selection, introduction, and notes on plates by Charles F. Ramus. Total of 158pp. 9⅜ x 12¼. 23512-2 Pa. $6.00

DRAWINGS OF MUCHA, Alphonse Maria Mucha. Work reveals draftsman of highest caliber: studies for famous posters and paintings, renderings for book illustrations and ads, etc. 70 works, 9 in color; including 6 items not drawings. Introduction. List of illustrations. 72pp. 9⅜ x 12¼. (Available in U.S. only) 23672-2 Pa. $4.00

GIOVANNI BATTISTA PIRANESI: DRAWINGS IN THE PIERPONT MORGAN LIBRARY, Giovanni Battista Piranesi. For first time ever all of Morgan Library's collection, world's largest. 167 illustrations of rare Piranesi drawings—archeological, architectural, decorative and visionary. Essay, detailed list of drawings, chronology, captions. Edited by Felice Stampfle. 144pp. 9⅜ x 12¼. 23714-1 Pa. $7.50

NEW YORK ETCHINGS (1905-1949), John Sloan. All of important American artist's N.Y. life etchings. 67 works include some of his best art; also lively historical record—Greenwich Village, tenement scenes. Edited by Sloan's widow. Introduction and captions. 79pp. 8⅜ x 11¼. 23651-X Pa. $4.00

CHINESE PAINTING AND CALLIGRAPHY: A PICTORIAL SURVEY, Wan-go Weng. 69 fine examples from John M. Crawford's matchless private collection: landscapes, birds, flowers, human figures, etc., plus calligraphy. Every basic form included: hanging scrolls, handscrolls, album leaves, fans, etc. 109 illustrations. Introduction. Captions. 192pp. 8⅞ x 11¾. 23707-9 Pa. $7.95

DRAWINGS OF REMBRANDT, edited by Seymour Slive. Updated Lippmann, Hofstede de Groot edition, with definitive scholarly apparatus. All portraits, biblical sketches, landscapes, nudes, Oriental figures, classical studies, together with selection of work by followers. 550 illustrations. Total of 630pp. 9⅛ x 12¼. 21485-0, 21486-9 Pa., Two-vol. set $15.00

THE DISASTERS OF WAR, Francisco Goya. 83 etchings record horrors of Napoleonic wars in Spain and war in general. Reprint of 1st edition, plus 3 additional plates. Introduction by Philip Hofer. 97pp. 9⅜ x 8¼. 21872-4 Pa. $4.00

THE DEPRESSION YEARS AS PHOTOGRAPHED BY ARTHUR ROTH-STEIN, Arthur Rothstein. First collection devoted entirely to the work of outstanding 1930s photographer: famous dust storm photo, ragged children, unemployed, etc. 120 photographs. Captions. 119pp. 9¼ x 10¾.
23590-4 Pa. $5.00

CAMERA WORK: A PICTORIAL GUIDE, Alfred Stieglitz. All 559 illustrations and plates from the most important periodical in the history of art photography, *Camera Work* (1903-17). Presented four to a page, reduced in size but still clear, in strict chronological order, with complete captions. Three indexes. Glossary. Bibliography. 176pp. 8⅜ x 11¼.
23591-2 Pa. $6.95

ALVIN LANGDON COBURN, PHOTOGRAPHER, Alvin L. Coburn. Revealing autobiography by one of greatest photographers of 20th century gives insider's version of Photo-Secession, plus comments on his own work. 77 photographs by Coburn. Edited by Helmut and Alison Gernsheim. 160pp. 8⅛ x 11.
23685-4 Pa. $6.00

NEW YORK IN THE FORTIES, Andreas Feininger. 162 brilliant photographs by the well-known photographer, formerly with *Life* magazine, show commuters, shoppers, Times Square at night, Harlem nightclub, Lower East Side, etc. Introduction and full captions by John von Hartz. 181pp. 9¼ x 10¾.
23585-8 Pa. $6.95

GREAT NEWS PHOTOS AND THE STORIES BEHIND THEM, John Faber. Dramatic volume of 140 great news photos, 1855 through 1976, and revealing stories behind them, with both historical and technical information. Hindenburg disaster, shooting of Oswald, nomination of Jimmy Carter, etc. 160pp. 8¼ x 11.
23667-6 Pa. $5.00

THE ART OF THE CINEMATOGRAPHER, Leonard Maltin. Survey of American cinematography history and anecdotal interviews with 5 masters—Arthur Miller, Hal Mohr, Hal Rosson, Lucien Ballard, and Conrad Hall. Very large selection of behind-the-scenes production photos. 105 photographs. Filmographies. Index. Originally *Behind the Camera*. 144pp. 8¼ x 11.
23686-2 Pa. $5.00

DESIGNS FOR THE THREE-CORNERED HAT (LE TRICORNE), Pablo Picasso. 32 fabulously rare drawings—including 31 color illustrations of costumes and accessories—for 1919 production of famous ballet. Edited by Parmenia Migel, who has written new introduction. 48pp. 9⅜ x 12¼. (Available in U.S. only)
23709-5 Pa. $5.00

NOTES OF A FILM DIRECTOR, Sergei Eisenstein. Greatest Russian filmmaker explains montage, making of *Alexander Nevsky*, aesthetics; comments on self, associates, great rivals (Chaplin), similar material. 78 illustrations. 240pp. 5⅜ x 8½.
22392-2 Pa. $4.50

CATALOGUE OF DOVER BOOKS

THE SENSE OF BEAUTY, George Santayana. Masterfully written discussion of nature of beauty, materials of beauty, form, expression; art, literature, social sciences all involved. 168pp. 5⅜ x 8½.   20238-0 Pa. $3.00

ON THE IMPROVEMENT OF THE UNDERSTANDING, Benedict Spinoza. Also contains *Ethics, Correspondence*, all in excellent R. Elwes translation. Basic works on entry to philosophy, pantheism, exchange of ideas with great contemporaries. 402pp. 5⅜ x 8½.   20250-X Pa. $4.50

THE TRAGIC SENSE OF LIFE, Miguel de Unamuno. Acknowledged masterpiece of existential literature, one of most important books of 20th century. Introduction by Madariaga. 367pp. 5⅜ x 8½.
20257-7 Pa. $4.50

THE GUIDE FOR THE PERPLEXED, Moses Maimonides. Great classic of medieval Judaism attempts to reconcile revealed religion (Pentateuch, commentaries) with Aristotelian philosophy. Important historically, still relevant in problems. Unabridged Friedlander translation. Total of 473pp. 5⅜ x 8½.   20351-4 Pa. $6.00

THE I CHING (THE BOOK OF CHANGES), translated by James Legge. Complete translation of basic text plus appendices by Confucius, and Chinese commentary of most penetrating divination manual ever prepared. Indispensable to study of early Oriental civilizations, to modern inquiring reader. 448pp. 5⅜ x 8½.   21062-6 Pa. $5.00

THE EGYPTIAN BOOK OF THE DEAD, E. A. Wallis Budge. Complete reproduction of Ani's papyrus, finest ever found. Full hieroglyphic text, interlinear transliteration, word for word translation, smooth translation. Basic work, for Egyptology, for modern study of psychic matters. Total of 533pp. 6½ x 9¼. (Available in U.S. only)   21866-X Pa. $5.95

THE GODS OF THE EGYPTIANS, E. A. Wallis Budge. Never excelled for richness, fullness: all gods, goddesses, demons, mythical figures of Ancient Egypt; their legends, rites, incarnations, variations, powers, etc. Many hieroglyphic texts cited. Over 225 illustrations, plus 6 color plates. Total of 988pp. 6⅛ x 9¼. (Available in U.S. only)
22055-9, 22056-7 Pa., Two-vol. set $16.00

THE STANDARD BOOK OF QUILT MAKING AND COLLECTING, Marguerite Ickis. Full information, full-sized patterns for making 46 traditional quilts, also 150 other patterns. Quilted cloths, lame, satin quilts, etc. 483 illustrations. 273pp. 6⅞ x 9⅝.   20582-7 Pa. $4.95

CORAL GARDENS AND THEIR MAGIC, Bronsilaw Malinowski. Classic study of the methods of tilling the soil and of agricultural rites in the Trobriand Islands of Melanesia. Author is one of the most important figures in the field of modern social anthropology. 143 illustrations. Indexes. Total of 911pp. of text. 5⅝ x 8¼. (Available in U.S. only)
23597-1 Pa. $12.95

THE ANATOMY OF THE HORSE, George Stubbs. Often considered the great masterpiece of animal anatomy. Full reproduction of 1766 edition, plus prospectus; original text and modernized text. 36 plates. Introduction by Eleanor Garvey. 121pp. 11 x 14¾.   23402-9 Pa. $6.00

BRIDGMAN'S LIFE DRAWING, George B. Bridgman. More than 500 illustrative drawings and text teach you to abstract the body into its major masses, use light and shade, proportion; as well as specific areas of anatomy, of which Bridgman is master. 192pp. 6½ x 9¼. (Available in U.S. only)
22710-3 Pa. $3.50

ART NOUVEAU DESIGNS IN COLOR, Alphonse Mucha, Maurice Verneuil, Georges Auriol. Full-color reproduction of *Combinaisons ornementales* (c. 1900) by Art Nouveau masters. Floral, animal, geometric, interlacings, swashes—borders, frames, spots—all incredibly beautiful. 60 plates, hundreds of designs. 9⅜ x 8-1/16.   22885-1 Pa. $4.00

FULL-COLOR FLORAL DESIGNS IN THE ART NOUVEAU STYLE, E. A. Seguy. 166 motifs, on 40 plates, from *Les fleurs et leurs applications decoratives* (1902): borders, circular designs, repeats, allovers, "spots." All in authentic Art Nouveau colors. 48pp. 9⅜ x 12¼.
23439-8 Pa. $5.00

A DIDEROT PICTORIAL ENCYCLOPEDIA OF TRADES AND IN-DUSTRY, edited by Charles C. Gillispie. 485 most interesting plates from the great French Encyclopedia of the 18th century show hundreds of working figures, artifacts, process, land and cityscapes; glassmaking, paper-making, metal extraction, construction, weaving, making furniture, clothing, wigs, dozens of other activities. Plates fully explained. 920pp. 9 x 12.
22284-5, 22285-3 Clothbd., Two-vol. set $40.00

HANDBOOK OF EARLY ADVERTISING ART, Clarence P. Hornung. Largest collection of copyright-free early and antique advertising art ever compiled. Over 6,000 illustrations, from Franklin's time to the 1890's for special effects, novelty. Valuable source, almost inexhaustible.
Pictorial Volume. Agriculture, the zodiac, animals, autos, birds, Christmas, fire engines, flowers, trees, musical instruments, ships, games and sports, much more. Arranged by subject matter and use. 237 plates. 288pp. 9 x 12.
20122-8 Clothbd. $14.50

Typographical Volume. Roman and Gothic faces ranging from 10 point to 300 point, "Barnum," German and Old English faces, script, logotypes, scrolls and flourishes, 1115 ornamental initials, 67 complete alphabets, more. 310 plates. 320pp. 9 x 12.   20123-6 Clothbd. $15.00

CALLIGRAPHY (CALLIGRAPHIA LATINA), J. G. Schwandner. High point of 18th-century ornamental calligraphy. Very ornate initials, scrolls, borders, cherubs, birds, lettered examples. 172pp. 9 x 13.
20475-8 Pa. $7.00

THE CURVES OF LIFE, Theodore A. Cook. Examination of shells, leaves, horns, human body, art, etc., in *"the* classic reference on how the golden ratio applies to spirals and helices in nature . . . . "—Martin Gardner. 426 illustrations. Total of 512pp. 5⅜ x 8½.   23701-X Pa. $5.95

AN ILLUSTRATED FLORA OF THE NORTHERN UNITED STATES AND CANADA, Nathaniel L. Britton, Addison Brown. Encyclopedic work covers 4666 species, ferns on up. Everything. Full botanical information, illustration for each. This earlier edition is preferred by many to more recent revisions. 1913 edition. Over 4000 illustrations, total of 2087pp. 6⅛ x 9¼.   22642-5, 22643-3, 22644-1 Pa., Three-vol. set $25.50

MANUAL OF THE GRASSES OF THE UNITED STATES, A. S. Hitchcock, U.S. Dept. of Agriculture. The basic study of American grasses, both indigenous and escapes, cultivated and wild. Over 1400 species. Full descriptions, information. Over 1100 maps, illustrations. Total of 1051pp. 5⅜ x 8½.   22717-0, 22718-9 Pa., Two-vol. set $15.00

THE CACTACEAE,, Nathaniel L. Britton, John N. Rose. Exhaustive, definitive. Every cactus in the world. Full botanical descriptions. Thorough statement of nomenclatures, habitat, detailed finding keys. The one book needed by every cactus enthusiast. Over 1275 illustrations. Total of 1080pp. 8 x 10¼.   21191-6, 21192-4 Clothbd., Two-vol. set $35.00

AMERICAN MEDICINAL PLANTS, Charles F. Millspaugh. Full descriptions, 180 plants covered: history; physical description; methods of preparation with all chemical constituents extracted; all claimed curative or adverse effects. 180 full-page plates. Classification table. 804pp. 6½ x 9¼.
23034-1 Pa. $12.95

A MODERN HERBAL, Margaret Grieve. Much the fullest, most exact, most useful compilation of herbal material. Gigantic alphabetical encyclopedia, from aconite to zedoary, gives botanical information, medical properties, folklore, economic uses, and much else. Indispensable to serious reader. 161 illustrations. 888pp. 6½ x 9¼. (Available in U.S. only)
22798-7, 22799-5 Pa., Two-vol. set $13.00

THE HERBAL or GENERAL HISTORY OF PLANTS, John Gerard. The 1633 edition revised and enlarged by Thomas Johnson. Containing almost 2850 plant descriptions and 2705 superb illustrations, Gerard's *Herbal* is a monumental work, the book all modern English herbals are derived from, the one herbal every serious enthusiast should have in its entirety. Original editions are worth perhaps $750. 1678pp. 8½ x 12¼.
23147-X Clothbd. $50.00

MANUAL OF THE TREES OF NORTH AMERICA, Charles S. Sargent. The basic survey of every native tree and tree-like shrub, 717 species in all. Extremely full descriptions, information on habitat, growth, locales, economics, etc. Necessary to every serious tree lover. Over 100 finding keys. 783 illustrations. Total of 986pp. 5⅜ x 8½.
20277-1, 20278-X Pa., Two-vol. set $11.00

THE EARLY WORK OF AUBREY BEARDSLEY, Aubrey Beardsley. 157 plates, 2 in color: *Manon Lescaut, Madame Bovary, Morte Darthur, Salome,* other. Introduction by H. Marillier. 182pp. 8⅛ x 11. 21816-3 Pa. $4.50

THE LATER WORK OF AUBREY BEARDSLEY, Aubrey Beardsley. Exotic masterpieces of full maturity: *Venus and Tannhauser, Lysistrata, Rape of the Lock, Volpone,* Savoy material, etc. 174 plates, 2 in color. 186pp. 8⅛ x 11. 21817-1 Pa. $5.95

THOMAS NAST'S CHRISTMAS DRAWINGS, Thomas Nast. Almost all Christmas drawings by creator of image of Santa Claus as we know it, and one of America's foremost illustrators and political cartoonists. 66 illustrations. 3 illustrations in color on covers. 96pp. 8⅜ x 11¼. 23660-9 Pa. $3.50

THE DORÉ ILLUSTRATIONS FOR DANTE'S DIVINE COMEDY, Gustave Doré. All 135 plates from Inferno, Purgatory, Paradise; fantastic tortures, infernal landscapes, celestial wonders. Each plate with appropriate (translated) verses. 141pp. 9 x 12. 23231-X Pa. $4.50

DORÉ'S ILLUSTRATIONS FOR RABELAIS, Gustave Doré. 252 striking illustrations of *Gargantua and Pantagruel* books by foremost 19th-century illustrator. Including 60 plates, 192 delightful smaller illustrations. 153pp. 9 x 12. 23656-0 Pa. $5.00

LONDON: A PILGRIMAGE, Gustave Doré, Blanchard Jerrold. Squalor, riches, misery, beauty of mid-Victorian metropolis; 55 wonderful plates, 125 other illustrations, full social, cultural text by Jerrold. 191pp. of text. 9⅜ x 12¼. 22306-X Pa. $7.00

THE RIME OF THE ANCIENT MARINER, Gustave Doré, S. T. Coleridge. Dore's finest work, 34 plates capture moods, subtleties of poem. Full text. Introduction by Millicent Rose. 77pp. 9¼ x 12. 22305-1 Pa. $3.50

THE DORE BIBLE ILLUSTRATIONS, Gustave Doré. All wonderful, detailed plates: Adam and Eve, Flood, Babylon, Life of Jesus, etc. Brief King James text with each plate. Introduction by Millicent Rose. 241 plates. 241pp. 9 x 12. 23004-X Pa. $6.00

THE COMPLETE ENGRAVINGS, ETCHINGS AND DRYPOINTS OF ALBRECHT DURER. "Knight, Death and Devil"; "Melencolia," and more—all Dürer's known works in all three media, including 6 works formerly attributed to him. 120 plates. 235pp. 8⅜ x 11¼. 22851-7 Pa. $6.50

MECHANICK EXERCISES ON THE WHOLE ART OF PRINTING, Joseph Moxon. First complete book (1683-4) ever written about typography, a compendium of everything known about printing at the latter part of 17th century. Reprint of 2nd (1962) Oxford Univ. Press edition. 74 illustrations. Total of 550pp. 6⅛ x 9¼. 23617-X Pa. $7.95

SECOND PIATIGORSKY CUP, edited by Isaac Kashdan. One of the greatest tournament books ever produced in the English language. All 90 games of the 1966 tournament, annotated by players, most annotated by both players. Features Petrosian, Spassky, Fischer, Larsen, six others. 228pp. 5⅜ x 8½.   23572-6 Pa. $3.50

ENCYCLOPEDIA OF CARD TRICKS, revised and edited by Jean Hugard. How to perform over 600 card tricks, devised by the world's greatest magicians: impromptus, spelling tricks, key cards, using special packs, much, much more. Additional chapter on card technique. 66 illustrations. 402pp. 5⅜ x 8½. (Available in U.S. only)   21252-1 Pa. $4.95

MAGIC: STAGE ILLUSIONS, SPECIAL EFFECTS AND TRICK PHOTOGRAPHY, Albert A. Hopkins, Henry R. Evans. One of the great classics; fullest, most authorative explanation of vanishing lady, levitations, scores of other great stage effects. Also small magic, automata, stunts. 446 illustrations. 556pp. 5⅜ x 8½.   23344-8 Pa. $6.95

THE SECRETS OF HOUDINI, J. C. Cannell. Classic study of Houdini's incredible magic, exposing closely-kept professional secrets and revealing, in general terms, the whole art of stage magic. 67 illustrations. 279pp. 5⅜ x 8½.   22913-0 Pa. $4.00

HOFFMANN'S MODERN MAGIC, Professor Hoffmann. One of the best, and best-known, magicians' manuals of the past century. Hundreds of tricks from card tricks and simple sleight of hand to elaborate illusions involving construction of complicated machinery. 332 illustrations. 563pp. 5⅜ x 8½.   23623-4 Pa. $6.00

MADAME PRUNIER'S FISH COOKERY BOOK, Mme. S. B. Prunier. More than 1000 recipes from world famous Prunier's of Paris and London, specially adapted here for American kitchen. Grilled tournedos with anchovy butter, Lobster a la Bordelaise, Prunier's prized desserts, more. Glossary. 340pp. 5⅜ x 8½. (Available in U.S. only)   22679-4 Pa. $3.00

FRENCH COUNTRY COOKING FOR AMERICANS, Louis Diat. 500 easy-to-make, authentic provincial recipes compiled by former head chef at New York's Fitz-Carlton Hotel: onion soup, lamb stew, potato pie, more. 309pp. 5⅜ x 8½.   23665-X Pa. $3.95

SAUCES, FRENCH AND FAMOUS, Louis Diat. Complete book gives over 200 specific recipes: bechamel, Bordelaise, hollandaise, Cumberland, apricot, etc. Author was one of this century's finest chefs, originator of vichyssoise and many other dishes. Index. 156pp. 5⅜ x 8.
23663-3 Pa. $2.75

TOLL HOUSE TRIED AND TRUE RECIPES, Ruth Graves Wakefield. Authentic recipes from the famous Mass. restaurant: popovers, veal and ham loaf, Toll House baked beans, chocolate cake crumb pudding, much more. Many helpful hints. Nearly 700 recipes. Index. 376pp. 5⅜ x 8½.
23560-2 Pa. $4.50

HISTORY OF BACTERIOLOGY, William Bulloch. The only comprehensive history of bacteriology from the beginnings through the 19th century. Special emphasis is given to biography-Leeuwenhoek, etc. Brief accounts of 350 bacteriologists form a separate section. No clearer, fuller study, suitable to scientists and general readers, has yet been written. 52 illustrations. 448pp. 5⅝ x 8¼. 23761-3 Pa. $6.50

THE COMPLETE NONSENSE OF EDWARD LEAR, Edward Lear. All nonsense limericks, zany alphabets, Owl and Pussycat, songs, nonsense botany, etc., illustrated by Lear. Total of 321pp. 5⅜ x 8½. (Available in U.S. only) 20167-8 Pa. $3.95

INGENIOUS MATHEMATICAL PROBLEMS AND METHODS, Louis A. Graham. Sophisticated material from Graham *Dial,* applied and pure; stresses solution methods. Logic, number theory, networks, inversions, etc. 237pp. 5⅜ x 8½. 20545-2 Pa. $4.50

BEST MATHEMATICAL PUZZLES OF SAM LOYD, edited by Martin Gardner. Bizarre, original, whimsical puzzles by America's greatest puzzler. From fabulously rare *Cyclopedia,* including famous 14-15 puzzles, the Horse of a Different Color, 115 more. Elementary math. 150 illustrations. 167pp. 5⅜ x 8½. 20498-7 Pa. $2.75

THE BASIS OF COMBINATION IN CHESS, J. du Mont. Easy-to-follow, instructive book on elements of combination play, with chapters on each piece and every powerful combination team—two knights, bishop and knight, rook and bishop, etc. 250 diagrams. 218pp. 5⅜ x 8½. (Available in U.S. only) 23644-7 Pa. $3.50

MODERN CHESS STRATEGY, Ludek Pachman. The use of the queen, the active king, exchanges, pawn play, the center, weak squares, etc. Section on rook alone worth price of the book. Stress on the moderns. Often considered the most important book on strategy. 314pp. 5⅜ x 8½. 20290-9 Pa. $4.50

LASKER'S MANUAL OF CHESS, Dr. Emanuel Lasker. Great world champion offers very thorough coverage of all aspects of chess. Combinations, position play, openings, end game, aesthetics of chess, philosophy of struggle, much more. Filled with analyzed games. 390pp. 5⅜ x 8½. 20640-8 Pa. $5.00

500 MASTER GAMES OF CHESS, S. Tartakower, J. du Mont. Vast collection of great chess games from 1798-1938, with much material nowhere else readily available. Fully annotated, arranged by opening for easier study. 664pp. 5⅜ x 8½. 23208-5 Pa. $7.50

A GUIDE TO CHESS ENDINGS, Dr. Max Euwe, David Hooper. One of the finest modern works on chess endings. Thorough analysis of the most frequently encountered endings by former world champion. 331 examples, each with diagram. 248pp. 5⅜ x 8½. 23332-4 Pa. $3.75

THE COMPLETE WOODCUTS OF ALBRECHT DURER, edited by Dr. W. Kurth. 346 in all: "Old Testament," "St. Jerome," "Passion," "Life of Virgin," Apocalypse," many others. Introduction by Campbell Dodgson. 285pp. 8½ x 12¼. 21097-9 Pa. $7.50

DRAWINGS OF ALBRECHT DURER, edited by Heinrich Wolfflin. 81 plates show development from youth to full style. Many favorites; many new. Introduction by Alfred Werner. 96pp. 8⅛ x 11. 22352-3 Pa. $5.00

THE HUMAN FIGURE, Albrecht Dürer. Experiments in various techniques—stereometric, progressive proportional, and others. Also life studies that rank among finest ever done. Complete reprinting of *Dresden Sketchbook*. 170 plates. 355pp. 8⅜ x 11¼. 21042-1 Pa. $7.95

OF THE JUST SHAPING OF LETTERS, Albrecht Dürer. Renaissance artist explains design of Roman majuscules by geometry, also Gothic lower and capitals. Grolier Club edition. 43pp. 7⅞ x 10¾ 21306-4 Pa. $3.00

TEN BOOKS ON ARCHITECTURE, Vitruvius. The most important book ever written on architecture. Early Roman aesthetics, technology, classical orders, site selection, all other aspects. Stands behind everything since. Morgan translation. 331pp. 5⅜ x 8½. 20645-9 Pa. $4.50

THE FOUR BOOKS OF ARCHITECTURE, Andrea Palladio. 16th-century classic responsible for Palladian movement and style. Covers classical architectural remains, Renaissance revivals, classical orders, etc. 1738 Ware English edition. Introduction by A. Placzek. 216 plates. 110pp. of text. 9½ x 12¾. 21308-0 Pa. $10.00

HORIZONS, Norman Bel Geddes. Great industrialist stage designer, "father of streamlining," on application of aesthetics to transportation, amusement, architecture, etc. 1932 prophetic account; function, theory, specific projects. 222 illustrations. 312pp. 7⅞ x 10¾. 23514-9 Pa. $6.95

FRANK LLOYD WRIGHT'S FALLINGWATER, Donald Hoffmann. Full, illustrated story of conception and building of Wright's masterwork at Bear Run, Pa. 100 photographs of site, construction, and details of completed structure. 112pp. 9¼ x 10. 23671-4 Pa. $5.50

THE ELEMENTS OF DRAWING, John Ruskin. Timeless classic by great Viltorian; starts with basic ideas, works through more difficult. Many practical exercises. 48 illustrations. Introduction by Lawrence Campbell. 228pp. 5⅜ x 8½. 22730-8 Pa. $3.75

GIST OF ART, John Sloan. Greatest modern American teacher, Art Students League, offers innumerable hints, instructions, guided comments to help you in painting. Not a formal course. 46 illustrations. Introduction by Helen Sloan. 200pp. 5⅜ x 8½. 23435-5 Pa. $4.00

AMERICAN ANTIQUE FURNITURE, Edgar G. Miller, Jr. The basic coverage of all American furniture before 1840: chapters per item chronologically cover all types of furniture, with more than 2100 photos. Total of 1106pp. 7⅞ x 10¾.   21599-7, 21600-4 Pa., Two-vol. set $17.90

ILLUSTRATED GUIDE TO SHAKER FURNITURE, Robert Meader. Director, Shaker Museum, Old Chatham, presents up-to-date coverage of all furniture and appurtenances, with much on local styles not available elsewhere. 235 photos. 146pp. 9 x 12.   22819-3 Pa. $6.00

ORIENTAL RUGS, ANTIQUE AND MODERN, Walter A. Hawley. Persia, Turkey, Caucasus, Central Asia, China, other traditions. Best general survey of all aspects: styles and periods, manufacture, uses, symbols and their interpretation, and identification. 96 illustrations, 11 in color. 320pp. 6⅛ x 9¼.   22366-3 Pa. $6.95

CHINESE POTTERY AND PORCELAIN, R. L. Hobson. Detailed descriptions and analyses by former Keeper of the Department of Oriental Antiquities and Ethnography at the British Museum. Covers hundreds of pieces from primitive times to 1915. Still the standard text for most periods. 136 plates, 40 in full color. Total of 750pp. 5⅝ x 8½.   23253-0 Pa. $10.00

THE WARES OF THE MING DYNASTY, R. L. Hobson. Foremost scholar examines and illustrates many varieties of Ming (1368-1644). Famous blue and white, polychrome, lesser-known styles and shapes. 117 illustrations, 9 full color, of outstanding pieces. Total of 263pp. 6⅛ x 9¼. (Available in U.S. only)   23652-8 Pa. $6.00

Prices subject to change without notice.

Available at your book dealer or write for free catalogue to Dept. GI, Dover Publications, Inc., 31 East Second Street, Mineola, N.Y. 11501. Dover publishes more than 175 books each year on science, elementary and advanced mathematics, biology, music, art, literary history, social sciences and other areas.